Drugs

Destruction

Divorce

Death

Divination

Deception

Dejection

Disobedience

Disease

Defilement

Depression

12

things
you don't
know
that could be
Destroying
YOU

By Dr. Sola Fola-Alade

12 THINGS YOU DON'T KNOW THAT COULD BE DESTROYING YOU

Copyright © Dr Sola Fola-Alade 2010

ISBN:978-0-9564767-4-6

Published by Vision Media Comm. Ltd
Email: info@colourdesigns.co.uk Tel: +44 7903 822 987

Printed in United Kingdom

Endorsements

Pastor Sola has done a good job of drawing the attention of the reader to the reality of present day spiritual warfare that confronts believers daily. It is a known legal principle that ignorance of the law is no defence. Similarly, ignorance of the existence of spiritual wars and invisible demonic militias that are behind such spiritual wars against believers can be fatal (Hosea 4:6).

Pastor Sola has demonstrated through his writing, the art of informed, strategic level of spiritual warfare that destroys compromised foundations in the lives of believers. Faulty foundations resulting from personal sin, generational curses, or strongholds in territories may attract usage or high volume traffic through demonic shuttles of Satanic militia. These satanic confederacies view lives, albeit born again, as landing stripes for curses (Proverbs 26:2).

I highly recommend this book as a day to day handbook and encourage readers to make good use of its practical approach to destroying foundational challenges. I would also like to endorse Pastor Sola as a marketplace apostle who is more interested in seeing God's kingdom advanced than empire building. It is with the heart of David that he indirectly questions through pages of this dynamic book; "is there not a cause?" With the courage of Samson, he has also exhibited in this book the response or reaction to the question asked thus; "there is a cause! But the thorns in the way must be destroyed."
All in all, a great read!

Obii Pax-Harry

The 12 D's identify the arsenal that the gates of hell have put out that not just all ministers of the gospel but all Christians should be cognisant of if they want to live Godly for Christ and experience the full manifestation of His glory.

Dr. Sola Fola-Alade has ingeniously, intuitively and perceptively identified, researched and collated information that every Christian must be aware of to seal the cracks in their spiritual armour and be fortified against; in these times of ever increasing iniquity.

I have had the privilege of knowing Pastor Sola for many years as a minister with great prophetic insight and foresight, which sees way ahead of the present times to forewarn and forearm the body of Christ in preparation for the storms we must all embrace in our walk up Mt. Zion.
Beyond that, I have watched him persevere through tests and trials, as he has endured these buffetings of hell that he so avidly describes in the 12 D's.

The 12 D's is not just a book of collated statistics, neither is it just intellectual assent to the scriptures, but beyond all that; it represents the experiences that this man of God has had to contend with and overcome to produce the anointing and cutting edge ministry that he currently exercises.

Dr. Sola Fola-Alade will be one of the Generals of the army of the Lord in times to come!

Watch out for him and the 12 D's.

Michael Adeyemi Adefarasin.

We are surrounded day by the day by an increase in the intensity, diversity and complexity of wickedness. Levels of wickedness, that is beyond the natural man's conception. Unseen forces are busy working their purposes and plans unrecognised and most times unhindered behind the scenes. This book unravels and exposes the cunning operations of the devil and the never ending glorious victory of Christ Jesus our Lord.

Thoughts are extraordinary streams that have invisible sources. When we fail to control our thoughts, the words and actions that proceed out of those thoughts can destroy us as demonic forces influence our thinking and consequently our actions. This book 12 things you don't know that could be destroying you by Dr Sola takes us on the journey of discovery to recovery. This is a must finish reading.

Apostle Dan Clad

ACKNOWLEDGEMENTS

I would like to say a big thank you to God for choosing, calling and empowering me to take on this assignment and fulfil this mandate and for sustaining and preserving me through it all.

Thanks to Tunde Adewumi who helped to oversee and keep the motivation going in the process of producing the book, and Bayo Awe who helped co-ordinate the print production.

I would like to thank those involved in the editing process, Taiwo Sofowora, Bisi Popoola, Kike Fadeyi & Ekwy Nnene.

Of course a big thank you to my wife Abimbola; for helping me rearrange the book and making it more readable; you are a rare gem.

I also want to thank my two lovely sons; you are my greatest "assets". Thanks for being patient with me as I wrote this book and for the many days I am away because of my ministry to others. You mean so much more to me than the work I do. I love you very much.

Book Dedication

I dedicate this book to my two wonderful sons, Toni and Tola. My favourite play mates. You are the motivation for what I do. May my ceiling in life become your own floor.

You are so much more important to me than the ministry.

PREFACE

L ife is not a walk in the park; it is more like a battleground. There is no demilitarised zone. You are either a friend of the enemy or a foe. Anyone who is not on the enemy's side is marked and open to attack. Those who take the battle of life casually will suffer many casualties.

Education and enlightenment have caused many to think that Satan is a myth. However, situations and circumstances around us say different. News headlines constantly report teenage murders, world epidemics, paedophilia, natural disasters, terrorism, wars, corruption in Government and the corporate world and continued liberalism in Government policies. These all testify to the world's inclination and propensity to lawlessness and evidence of an evil mastermind pulling the strings.

Satan cannot be everywhere unlike God Almighty who is Omnipresent, Omniscient and Omnipotent. Therefore, Satan has to work through a highly organised army (*'every kingdom divided against itself will not stand'*) of fallen spirits, called demons (*'for we do not wrestle against flesh and blood, but against principalities, against powers, against the rulers of the darkness of this age, against spiritual hosts of wickedness in the heavenly places'*).

As the church is broken down into departments and small groups, the army is also organised into corps. The signal corps handles communication; foot soldiers manage ground forces; troops implement strategy; armour corps for weaponry and so on.

Satan's army is also co-ordinated through a chain of command. As there are lower ranking individual troops who implement strategy, there are also senior ranking officers who devise and plan strategy against nations, cities, communities, families and individuals. Remember that we should *'keep Satan from getting the advantage over us; for we are not ignorant of his wiles and intentions.'* It is also important to *'wage war through wise counsel.'*

A roaring lion seeking whom to devour

Anything that steals, kills and destroys our abundant and fruitful life in Christ is a weapon formed and fashioned by our arch-enemy Satan.

Your invisible enemies (demons) fight dirty

1 Matthew 12:25
2 Ephesians 6:12
3 2 Corinthians 2:11 AMP
4 Proverbs 20:18

We would be wise to note that demons do not play fight. The following points drawn from the story of the boy possessed with an evil spirit will illustrate this:

- They try to disrupt God's plan and destroy His authority, showing their sense of defiance. It was when the evil spirit saw Jesus that he threw the boy into a convulsion (Mark 9:20).
- They make people do unusual things, not caring about the disgrace they bring on these people. When the evil spirit made the boy foam from the mouth, it did not regard that he would be embarrassed by the stares of people present there (v. 20).
- They attack from childhood. It is interesting that Jesus asked the boy's father how long the boy had been like that - he had been

possessed since childhood (v. 21).

- They try to destroy people by causing accidents. The boy's father told Jesus stories of how he had been thrown by the spirit into the fire on some occasions and into the water on others (v. 22).
- They are resistant; they never want to leave the individual, family or region and always seek to return, which is why Jesus added the clause, *'Enter him no more'*. (v. 25).

In this book, we explore and expose some of his chief weapons arsenaled against this generation - his weapons of Mass Destruction and show you how to gain victory!

CONTENTS

INTRODUCTION

INSIDE THE MIND OF THE ENEMY

*"The thief comes only in order to steal and kill and destroy.
I came that they may have and enjoy life and have it in
abundance" (to the full, till it overflows) (John 10:10).*

In order to win this battle, it is important to be aware of the
workings of the mind of the enemy.

DEMONS ON ASSIGNMENT

*19 Then Micaiah said, "Therefore hear the word of the LORD: I
saw the LORD sitting on His throne and all the host of heaven
standing by, on His right hand and on His left. 20 And the LORD
said, 'Who will persuade Ahab to go up, that he may fall at Ramoth
Gilead?' So one spoke in this manner and another spoke in that
manner. 21 Then a spirit came forward and stood before the LORD
and said, 'I will persuade him.' 22 The LORD said to him, 'In what
way?' So he said, 'I will go out and be a lying spirit in the mouth of
all his prophets.' And the LORD said, 'You shall persuade him and
also prevail. Go out and do so.' 23 Therefore look! The LORD has
put a lying spirit in the mouth of all these prophets of yours and the
LORD has declared disaster against you" (1 Kings 22: 19-23).*

The above scripture indicates that God, the Father of all spirits, employs the use of spirits to achieve His purposes and since Satan's eternal desire is to be like God, he also copies God's strategies. He uses demonic spirits to entice, deceive and destroy people he has profiled and targeted for destruction.

Satan has an array of demonic spirits at his beck and call and sometimes uses a combination of spirits to deal a blow and achieve his evil agenda e.g. spirits of deception (lying spirits), seduction, rejection and betrayal can work together.

DEMONS FROM BIRTH

From the womb to the tomb, Satan diligently sets out to obscure one's ability to grow spiritually, mentally, physically and emotionally in this life. A preacher I know once had a vision. He saw that demons were assigned to babies as they were born in the hospital. The demons attached themselves to the spirit of the child to ensure their growth and morality was hampered in some way.

Perhaps you have wondered why this generation has produced so many unsavoury characters and a higher degree of immorality compared to other generations, or the reason there are more people on drugs, into violence, illicit relationships, scandalous and disgraceful living. One reason is the devil fears that a 'deliverer' is about to be birthed again. What is more, he knows that this is not just one deliverer, but a body of deliverers!

BRINGING DOWN STRONG MEN

If the enemy wants to destroy a nation, he begins by identifying the strongest man who is most likely to be the leader. A quote by Sun

Tzu points out that it is wise to win the battle using as little resources as possible.

Once he has identified this key person, he releases his entire arsenal on that man or woman. If he wins the battle, it confirms that, 'when someone stronger [than the strong man] attacks and overpowers him, he takes away the armour which the man puts his trust in and divides up his spoils.'

Satan, a long-term strategist, has foresight and uses this to identify the strong man, as well as to start his destructive work even before the strong man is born. For example, the devil knew that Israel was to be delivered from the land of Egypt after 400 years of captivity; therefore, he calculated that the deliverer would be born round about the time that Moses was born. He tried to terminate Moses' life by using the River Nile.

Another classic example of this is the advent of Jesus Christ. Satan knew of this when the three wise men said they had seen the star. When the devil discerned that it would be around that time that the Saviour of the world would be born, Herod declared that all the boys in Bethlehem and its environs around the age of two and under should Pharaoh twice to declare that every male offspring of the Israelites should be killed; first through the midwives right on the birthing stool and when that failed, by throwing them into be killed. The question is: Could you be God's next strong man or woman? If you are, you need to be aware that somebody you don't want is probably watching you.

HIGH LEVEL SATANIC STRATEGIES

"...lest Satan should take advantage of us; for we are not ignorant

of his devices". (2 Corinthians 2:11).

I recently embarked on a journey in the scriptures to walk in the footsteps of Jesus by studying the four gospels over 90 days. I made some further interesting discoveries about Satan's strategies to destroy us and God's plans, methods and purpose to preserve and protect us from the enemy's devices. These discoveries will teach us a thing or two about the way the enemy operates and how, if we are sensitive to God's Spirit, we are always two steps ahead of the enemy's plans. They are outlined as follows.

Chapter 2 of the book of Matthew is one of my favourite chapters because it shows us that God speaks to us in different ways e.g. prophecy, scripture (recorded prophecy), dreams, wise men's counsel and circumstances (The Star).

A. *Matthew 2:1* indicates that it is only wise and discerning men that can see an individual's star potential while he is in the "manger". All others will only know who he really is when he has already manifested.

"After Jesus was born in Bethlehem in Judea, during the time of King Herod, Magi from the east came to Jerusalem and asked, 'Where is the one who has been born king of the Jews? <u>We saw his star</u> in the east and have come to worship him.'"

B. *Matthew 2:3* - Some people are troubled by the rising of another's Star (Potential).

---

[1]The Art of War, by Sun Tzu
[2]Luke 11:22
[3]Exodus 1:15-22
[4]Matthew 2:16

"When <u>King Herod heard</u> this <u>he was disturbed</u> and all Jerusalem with him."

C. *Matthew 2:4* shows the enemy does some satanic surveillance on God's children destined for greatness and seeks to destroy them.

"4. When he had called together all the people's chief priests and teachers of the law, <u>he asked them where the Christ was to be born.</u>

D. *Matthew 2:5* confirms that God reveals to prophets important and significant events long time before they happen.

"5. In Bethlehem of Judea," they replied, "<u>for this is what the prophet has written:"</u> 6'But you, Bethlehem, in the land of Judah, are by no means least among the rulers of Judah; for out of you will come a ruler who will be the shepherd of my people Israel.'"

E. *Matthew 2:7* shows that Herod used scripture (prophetic records) and the counsel of Wise men to locate a destined child for his evil purpose; you should be able to use the same to locate your destiny for good and for God's purpose.

7Then Herod called the Magi secretly and found out from them the exact time the star had appeared. 8. He sent them to Bethlehem and said, '<u>Go and make a careful search for the child</u>. As soon as you find him, <u>report to me</u>, so that I too may go and worship him.'"

F. *Matthew 2:12, 13, 19, 22* highlight the significance of dreams in the leadings of God even though not all dreams are significant. The Holy Spirit warns or instructs through dreams on four different occasions in this chapter alone.

"12 And having been warned in a <u>dream </u>not to go back to Herod,

they returned to their country by another route." 13 When they had gone, an angel of the Lord appeared to Joseph in a <u>dream</u>. "Get up," he said, "take the child and his mother and escape to Egypt. Stay there until I tell you, for Herod is going to search for the child to kill him." 14 So he got up, took the child and his mother during the night and left for Egypt, 15 where he stayed until the death of Herod." 19 After Herod died, an angel of the Lord appeared in a <u>dream </u>to Joseph in Egypt 20 and said, "Get up, take the child and his mother and go to the land of Israel, for those who were trying to take the child's life are dead."

21 So he got up took the child and his mother and went to the land of Israel. 22 But when he heard that Archelaus was reigning in Judea in place of his father Herod, he was afraid to go there. Having been warned in a <u>dream</u>, he withdrew to the district of Galilee, 23 and he went and lived in a town called Nazareth. So was fulfilled what was said through the prophets: "He will be called a Nazarene."

G. *Matthew 2:16-17* shows Satan will go to any length to destroy Divine destiny.

"16 When Herod realized that he had been outwitted by the Magi, he was furious and <u>he gave orders to kill all the boys</u> in Bethlehem and its vicinity who were two years old and under, in accordance with the time he had learned from the Magi. 17 Then what was said through the prophet Jeremiah was fulfilled:"

H. *Matthew 2:21-23* show that God orders our steps and will even choose and reveal where we ought to live in order to fulfil His Divine plan and for our own preservation.

"21So he got up took the child and his mother and went to the land

of Israel. 22But when he heard that Archelaus was reigning in Judea in place of his father Herod, he was afraid to go there. <u>Having been warned in a dream</u>, he withdrew to the district of <u>Galilee</u>, 23and he went and lived in a town called Nazareth. So was fulfilled what was said through the prophets: 'He will be called a Nazarene.'"

DEMONIC (SATANIC) PROFILING

4When he had called together all the people's chief priests and teachers of the law, <u>he asked them where the Christ was to be born.</u> 5"In Bethlehem in Judea," they replied, "for this is what the prophet has written: 6'But you, Bethlehem, in the land of Judah, are by no means least among the rulers of Judah; for out of you will come a ruler who will be the shepherd of my people Israel.'

7Then Herod called the Magi <u>secretly and found out from them the exact time the star had appeared.</u> 8He sent them to Bethlehem and said, "Go and <u>make a careful search for the child. As soon as you find him, report to me,</u> so that I too may go and worship him" (Matthew 2:4-8).

From the scripture above and the prior section, it is quite evident that Satan and his cohorts profile people destined for great things with God and assigns surveillance agents to track, locate and submit reports on these individuals' lives in order to plot demonic assaults and conspiracies.

The enemy does not only plot a demographic and geographic profile of our lives but also a psychographic profile which will indicate our likes and dislikes, strengths and weaknesses, habits and routines.

Psychographic profiling is used by many companies to understand the buying patterns and sometimes to trace the movements and routines of customers in order to target-market them with products that are most suited to their identified needs from their buying patterns. This is why many supermarkets and airlines have a reward card that is swiped at the check-out counter after every purchase. This information is accumulated, collated and then analysed on a computer program to plot each customer's peculiar buying pattern. Intelligence services can also use your credit card purchases to identify one's present location and use that information to trail wanted individuals.

In the same way, Satan profiles people in order to assign demonic agents to set them up to fail, fall or for complete destruction.

SAMSON'S DEMONIC PROFILE

"Afterward it happened that he loved a woman in the Valley of Sorek, whose name was Delilah.

5 And the lords of the Philistines came up to her and said to her, "Entice him and find out where his great strength lies and by what means we may overpower him, that we may bind him to afflict him; and every one of us will give you eleven hundred pieces of silver."" *(Judges 16:4, 5).*

In the case of Samson, instead of the Philistines going to war with the Israelites, they carried out espionage and discovered who the strong man in Israel was. They conducted some surveillance and it was not long before they revealed that his weakness was women. They were then able to work through this weakness (women) to discover that his strength was in his long hair and to cut off the source of his strength.

How Does The Devil Get Through To People? (Understanding Curses, Patterns and Assignments)

Sins and curses

Sin and curses are the commonest avenues through which demonic spirits gain entry to operate demonic assignments and set up satanic appointments. These assignments are empowered by evil spirits who implement the objective of the curse and perpetuate their wicked intentions. Satan's activities can be particularly deadly when he has both sin and curses to work with.

As you read on, remember demonic spirits do not work or operate in an ad-hoc or haphazard way, they are quite strategic and specific and operate in cycles and patterns.

Curses

What is a Curse?

A curse is an invocation of spiritual powers that marks an individual, family or people out for injury, hindrance or destruction. According to Dr. Joe Ibojie[1], "A curse is a pronouncement or a spoken word that has some particular form of spiritual power and or authority to bring limitation on a target. A curse is empowered by an evil spirit which implements the objective of the curse."

Apostle John Eckhardt[2] says, "A curse is God's recompense in the life of a person and he or her descendants as a result of iniquity. The curse causes sorrow of heart and gives demonic spirits legal entry into a family whereby they can carry out and perpetuate their wicked devices."

THE EFFECTS OF A CURSE

"Render unto them recompense, O Lord, according to the work of their hands. Give them sorrow of heart, thy curse unto them. Persecute and destroy them in anger from under the heavens of the Lord" (Lamentations 3:64-66).

According to Apostle John Eckhardt[3] the following words reveal the dynamics and outworking of a curse (i.e. a person who is cursed will experience all or some of the following).

- **Recompense** means reward or what is due to someone based on certain events or behaviour. A cursed person receives punishment or reward for wrong actions of theirs or those of ancestors.

- **Iniquity** means a very wrong and unfair action or situation. A cursed person will often experience a variety of actions or find themselves in situations that are unfair.

- **Perversion** the changing of something so that it is not what it was or should be or sexual behaviour which is considered strange and unpleasant by most people. A cursed person may find himself indulging or desiring to indulge in behaviour that is strange or perverse.

- **Persecution** means to harass in a manner designed to injure, grieve, or afflict; to pester; to run after with hostile intent; chase; put to flight; follow after; hunt; pursue. A cursed person will often feel like prey – hunted down, pursued and overcome.

- **Destruction** The action or process of destroying something by terminating it or causing so much damage to it that it cannot be repaired or no longer exists or be usable or to render utterly useless. Sometimes, the effects of a curse are so severe that it is almost irreparable.

GENERATIONAL PATTERNS AND DEMONIC CYCLES

Generational patterns are sins or curses repeated across generations, but a demonic cycle is the repetition of a sin or curse at set intervals or seasons within the same generation. Before we look at examples of generational patterns and demonic cycles, let's have a quick look at triggers for demonic cycles and curses.

TRIGGERS FOR DEMONIC CURSES AND CYCLES

Like the sparrow in her wandering, like the swallow in her flying, so the <u>causeless</u> curse does not <u>alight</u>. (Proverbs 26:2)

---

[1] Ibojie, Joe Dr., (2006), How to live the supernatural life in the here and now (Destiny Image)

[2] Eckhardt, John Apostle, (1920) Identifying and Breaking Curses (Whitaker House)

[3] Eckhardt, John Apostle, (1920) Identifying and Breaking Curses (Whitaker House)

Dr. Joe Ibojie in his book "*How to live the Supernatural life in the here and now*", stated that certain things trigger dormant curses into activity. He says curses can be

1. **Time sensitive** - The Bible in *Deuteronomy 28* says "*...when you go out...*"
2. **Location specific** - "*... cursed in the city ... cursed in the field...*"
3. **Gender specific** - "*.... barrenness of the womb...*"
4. **Situation sensitive** - "*... You shall <u>betroth a wife</u>, but another man shall lie with her; you shall <u>build a house</u>, but not live in it; you shall <u>plant a vineyard,</u> but not gather its grapes...*" *Deuteronomy 28:30.*
5. **Age sensitive** - the curse on Eli's family in 1 Samuel 2:30.

The list above shows that curses can be triggered at certain times, in certain locations or in certain situations. Some curses are also gender specific or age specific. Now, let's have a closer look at examples of generational and cyclical curses.

GENERATIONAL CURSES

THE DEATH OF ELI'S CHILDREN'S CHILDREN

In the scriptures below we see an example of how a sin opens the door to a curse and provokes judgment and then becomes a generational pattern.

THE CAUSE OF THE CURSE

"In that day I will perform against Eli all that I have spoken concerning his house, from beginning to end.

13 "For I have told him that I will judge his house forever for the iniquity which he knows, because his sons made themselves vile and he did not restrain them.

14 "And therefore I have sworn to the house of Eli that the iniquity of Eli's house shall not be atoned for by sacrifice or offering forever." (1Samuel 3:12-14)

25 "If one man sins against another, God will judge him. But if a man sins against the LORD, who will intercede for him?" Nevertheless they did not heed the voice of their father, because the LORD desired to kill them…

29 'Why do you kick at My sacrifice and My offering which I have commanded in My dwelling place and honour your sons more than Me, to make yourselves fat with the best of all the offerings of Israel My people?'

30 "Therefore the LORD God of Israel says: 'I said indeed that your house and the house of your father would walk before Me forever.' But now the LORD says: 'Far be it from Me; for those who honour Me I will honour and those who despise Me shall be lightly esteemed.

31 'Behold, the days are coming that I will cut off your arm and the arm of your father's house, so that there will not be an old man in your house.

32 'And you will see an enemy in My dwelling place, despite all the good which God does for Israel. And there shall not be an old man in your house forever.

33 'But any of your men whom I do not cut off from My altar shall *consume your eyes and grieve your heart. <u>And all the descendants of your house shall die in the flower of their age.</u>*

34 'Now this shall be a sign to you that will come upon <u>your two sons, on Hophni and Phinehas: in one day they shall die, both of them.</u>" (1 Samuel 2:25, 29-34)

The Judgment or Enforcement of the Curse

"17 So the messenger answered and said, "Israel has fled before the Philistines and there has been a great slaughter among the people. Also your <u>two sons, Hophni and Phinehas, are dead</u>; and the ark of God has been captured."18 Then it happened, when he made mention of the ark of God, that <u>Eli fell off the seat backward by the side of the gate; and his neck was broken and he died, for the man was old and heavy</u>. And he had judged Israel forty years.

19 Now his daughter-in-law, Phinehas' wife, was with child, due to be delivered; and when she heard the news that the ark of God was captured and that her father-in-law and her husband were dead, she bowed herself and gave birth, for her labour pains came upon her.

20 And <u>about the time of her death</u> the women who stood by her said to her, "Do not fear, for you have borne a son." <u>But she did not answer,</u> nor did she regard it.

We see in the above scriptures how an assignment of death was released over the house of Eli for generations due to their sin and how swiftly and effectively it was executed.

Generational Patterns and Curses

Scripture shows a few examples of how demonic patterns occur along family bloodlines. One of such is the example of Abraham and Isaac lying about their wives. Abraham first lied to Pharaoh and then at a later time he repeated the same act of lying to Abimelech.

Abraham lies to Pharaoh

Why did you say, <u>She is my sister,</u> so that I took her to be my wife? Now then, here is your wife; take her and get away [from here]! (Genesis 12:19)

Abraham lies to Abimelech

When God caused me to wander from my father's house, I said to her, this kindness you can show me: at every place we stop, say of me, <u>He is my brother</u> (Genesis 20:13).

Isaac lies to Abimelech

And the men of the place asked him about his wife and he said, <u>She is my sister;</u> for he was afraid to say, She is my wife--[thinking], Lest the men of the place should kill me for Rebekah, because she is attractive and is beautiful to look upon (Genesis 26:7).

From the last scripture we see how these demonic cycles can cross from one generation to another and become generational cycles or patterns. There are plenty of modern day examples of generational patterns and curses.

THE 30 YEAR CYCLE

A certain lady was singled out by a guest prophet who revealed that her daughter's carer had cast a witchcraft spell on her daughter to inflict a fatal illness; he then went on to unveil that the same thing was done to her by her carer about 30 years previously, which the lady also confirmed. This is an example of a generational cycle or bloodline pattern. Demonic assignments travel through family lines and like profiles, these patterns can also be traced.

BRUCE LEE'S CYCLE OF DEATH

The movie 'Dragon: The Bruce Lee story' is one of the best secular examples of a generational pattern and demonic assignment. Bruce Lee's father had informed him about an ancient demon in the family that would come to wrestle with the men of the family for their life; and many hadn't survived. In an effort to deceive this ancient demon, Bruce Lee was dressed up as a girl when he was a child! Obviously he couldn't continue the disguise into adulthood and as an adult he would wrestle with this demon time and again. Several times on his movie sets he would be disoriented and dazed for a few minutes when he would experience very real (to him) physical interaction/fights with this larger than life beast – that nobody else could see or experience. He eventually died on a film set at a very young age in the prime of his career, perpetuating the family pattern of early male deaths. His son, Brandon Lee also died mysteriously on a film set at a young age at the start of a glittering career a generation later.

CYCLICAL CURSES

Judges 6:3 is an example of a demonic cyclical curse. This occurs when certain sins or curses manifest seasonally for example every 5, 7, or 10 years or at specific life seasons.

For whenever Israel had sown their seed, the Midianites and the Amalekites and the people of the east came up against them.

The Lincoln-Kennedy pattern
I discovered an interesting piece on the internet[4] that helps to further illustrate the mysterious principle of cyclical curses and patterns.

Abraham Lincoln was elected to Congress in 1846.
John F. Kennedy was elected to Congress in 1946

Lincoln failed to win the Vice Presidential nomination in 1856.
Kennedy failed to win the Vice Presidential nomination in 1956.

Abraham Lincoln was elected President in 1860.
John F. Kennedy was elected President in 1960.

Lincoln defeated Stephen Douglas who was born in 1813.
Kennedy defeated Richard Nixon who was born in 1913.

Both were particularly concerned with civil rights.

Both had wives who lost children while in the White House.

Both Presidents were shot on a Friday.

---

[12] Wikipedia, Lincoln-Kennedy coincidences urban legend

Both Presidents were shot in the head.

Both were assassinated by Southerners.

Both were succeeded by Southerners.

Both Presidents had Vice Presidents named Johnson.

Lincoln's Vice President was called Andrew Johnson and he served in the House of Representatives in 1847. Kennedy's Vice President was called Lyndon Johnson and he served in the House of Representatives in 1947.

Andrew Johnson, who succeeded Lincoln, was born in 1808.
Lyndon Johnson, who succeeded Kennedy, was born in 1908

John Wilkes Booth, who assassinated Lincoln, was born in 1838. (Not 1839)!
Lee Harvey Oswald, who assassinated Kennedy, was born in 1939.

Both assassins were known by the three names.
Both names are composed of fifteen letters.

Lincoln was shot at the theatre called "Ford".
Kennedy was shot in a car named "Lincoln", made by Ford.

Booth ran from the theatre and was caught in a warehouse.
Oswald ran from a warehouse and was caught in a theatre.

Booth and Oswald were assassinated before their trials.

President Lincoln was born on February 12, 1809 and died on April 15, 1865 (age 56)

President Kennedy was born on May 29, 1917 and died on November 22, 1963 (age 46)

Merely a coincidence? You decide.

THE AMERICAN PRESIDENTS' TIPPECANOE CURSE

Here's yet another interesting historic discovery on the internet on the power of demonic cycles and patterns in the execution of curses.

The following was culled from *Wikipedia*:
"The curse, first widely noted in a Ripley's *Believe It or Not* book published in 1931,[1] began with the death of William Henry Harrison, who died in 1841 after having been elected in 1840. **For the next 120 years, presidents elected during years ending in a zero (occurring every 20 years) ultimately died while serving in office, from Harrison to John F. Kennedy (elected 1960, died 1963).**

The name "Curse of Tippecanoe" derives from the 1811 battle. As governor of the Indiana Territory, William Harrison bribed Native Americans to cede their lands to the U.S. government and handed out whiskey, causing problems for the Indians. These hostile acts angered the Shawnee chief Tecumseh and brought government soldiers and Native Americans to the brink of war in a period known as Tecumseh's War. Tecumseh and his brother organized a defensive group of Indian tribes designed to resist white westward expansion. In 1811, Harrison successfully attacked Tecumseh's village along the Tippecanoe River, earning fame and the nickname "Old Tippecanoe". Harrison strengthened his reputation even more by defeating the British at the Battle of the Thames during the War of 1812. Tecumseh's brother Tenskwatawa, known as the Prophet, supposedly set a curse against Harrison and future White House occupants who became president during years with the same end number as Harrison.

After the observation by Ripley, talk of the curse resurfaced as the next cursed election year approached. A similar oddities cartoon feature, 'Strange As it Seems' by John Hix, appeared prior to Election Day 1940, with "CURSE OVER THE WHITE HOUSE!" A list, running from "1840 - Harrison" to "1920 - Harding" was followed by (another) note (stating) that "In the last 100 years, Every U.S. President Elected at 20-Year Intervals Has Died In Office!" Ed Koterba, author of a syndicated column called "Assignment Washington", referred to the subject again in 1960.
As 1980 approached, the curse was sufficiently well-known and Americans wondered whether the winner of that election would follow the pattern." Ronald Reagan was elected president in 1980 and an assassination attempt was made on his life in 1981.

REPEATED CYCLES OF SIN OR BLESSINGS

In almost two decades of counselling, I have come across a number of generational patterns and a few demonic cycles in people's lives. I have seen particular sins repeat themselves in an individual's life every 5, 7 or 10 years apart. On a more positive note, a Pastor friend of mine has noticed a pattern of having to change locations every 7 years.

Satanic Appointments

An appointment by definition is a meeting set for a specific time and place.

A Satanic appointment is one set by evil demonic agencies to mark or target an individual for an evil activity at a specific place and time. This appointment is often based on the demonic profile garnered from studying the individual's routines, rituals, patterns and lifestyle over time.

"It came to pass at that time that Judah <u>departed from his brothers and visited a certain Adullamite whose name was Hirah.</u>

2 And Judah saw there a daughter of a certain Canaanite whose name was Shua and he married her and went in to her.

3 So she conceived and bore a son and he called his name Er…

…12 Now in the process of time the daughter of Shua, Judah's wife, died; and Judah was comforted and went up to his sheepshearers at Timnah, <u>he and his friend Hirah the Adullamite.</u>

13 And <u>it was told Tamar,</u> saying, <u>"Look, your father-in-law is going up to Timnah to shear his sheep."</u>

14 So she took off her widow's garments, covered herself with a veil and wrapped herself and sat in an open place which was on the way to Timnah; for she saw that Shelah was grown and she was not given to him as a wife.

15 When Judah saw her, <u>he thought she was a harlot, because she had covered her face.</u>

16 Then he turned to her by the way and said, "Please let me come in to you"; for he did not know that she was his daughter-in-law. So she said, "What will you give me that you may come in to me?"

17 And he said, "I will send a young goat from the flock." So she said, "Will you give me a pledge till you send it?"

18 Then he said, "What pledge shall I give you?" So she said, "Your signet and cord and your staff that is in your hand." Then he gave them to her and went in to her and she conceived by him.

19 So she arose and went away and laid aside her veil and put on the garments of her widowhood.

20 And Judah sent the young goat by the hand of his friend the Adullamite, to receive his pledge from the woman's hand, but he did not find her.

21 Then he asked the men of that place, saying, "Where is the harlot who was openly by the roadside?" And they said, "There was no harlot in this place."

22 So he returned to Judah and said, "I cannot find her. Also, the men of the place said there was no harlot in this place" (Genesis 38).

The above scripture demonstrates the classic dynamics of a satanic appointment.

In it, we see how Tamar had noticed from studying Judah over time that he had a proclivity towards foreign women (which was a sin at the time) and a habit of picking up girls when he left his brothers and went to visit his friend Hiram the Adullamite. With this information or profile in hand she knew his weakness and devised a Satanic strategy to pose and position herself as a harlot at a particular place and time on his usual route. In the same way many great men and women have been brought down and destroyed through satanic appointments that resulted in illicit activity.

DEMONIC ASSIGNMENTS

"<u>God sent a spirit of ill will</u> between Abimelech and the men of Shechem; and the men of Shechem dealt treacherously with Abimelech,

24 that the crime done to the seventy sons of Jerubbaal might be settled and their blood be laid on Abimelech their brother, who killed them and on the men of Shechem, who aided him in the killing of his brothers.
25 And the men of Shechem set men in ambush against him on the tops of the mountains and they robbed all who passed by them along that way; and it was told Abimelech" (Judges 9:22-25).

This is the enforcement and execution of the consequences or objectives of a curse by an assigned demonic spirit. They operate like police officers given a warrant for one's arrest or a bailiff empowered by the magistrate to strip an individual of all his goods in order to pay a debt. Their focus is like that of a guided missile that is locked on its target until it finds, hits and destroys its set object causing death, disease, divorce or defilement or one of the other demonic assignments discussed in the chapters to follow.

These spirits do not relent until they perform their assigned duties or until someone intercedes and God mercifully intervenes.

AFFLICTION WILL NOT ARISE A SECOND TIME

I have identified 12 demonic spirits and strategies that the enemy uses against this generation but they are, by no means, an exhaustive list. From my observation, they seem to be the chief weapons that Satan wields against this generation – to frustrate, denigrate and if possible extinguish many. In the following chapters we will elaborate on these 12 demonic assignments. But do not despair, you will also be equipped to battle and overcome them in Jesus name! Amen.

SECTION 1

LIFE EXTINGUISHERS

CHAPTER ONE

DEATH

THE FACTS

- In the year 2005, 16.4% of babies died for unascertained reasons before they reached the age of 28 days in the UK. [5]
- Leading causes of death in the Western world in descending order are heart disease, stroke, chest infections, lung cancer, car accidents and suicide.[6]
- Cancer is a leading cause of deaths worldwide: it accounted for 7.4 million deaths (around 13% of all deaths) in 2004.[7]
- More than 30% of cancer deaths can be prevented.[8]
- More than 70% of all cancer deaths occurred in low and middle income countries.[9]
- Deaths from cancer worldwide are projected to continue rising, with an estimated 12 million deaths in 2030 (World Health Organisation (WHO) report).[10]

Death is the total annihilation of the individual. It is the highest and ultimate plan of the enemy for the individual, so that they do not fulfil their destiny.

If he can prematurely terminate one's destiny, then he has stopped that individual from being able to fulfil the plan of God for their life.

Death can also mean a separation from God in life because to exist without God is death. The enemy's ultimate plan is to ensure that as many people as go through life die without the knowledge of God. This to counteract God's plan who is *'not willing that any should perish but that all should come to repentance"*. His plan is to cause mankind to live a life of continuous or abject sin which leads to separation from God. The enemy rejoices when individuals live and die not knowing God at all, leading them to total and eternal separation from God and into a place of eternal damnation – hell; but when he cannot achieve this, for those who have come to discern God, he tries to terminate their lives in order to ensure that they do not fulfil their God-given destinies.

YOUR APPOINTMENT WITH DEATH

Every individual has an appointment with death. Every man has a certain and definite appointment with death, *'as it is appointed for men to die once and after this, judgment.'* Satan tries to terminate a person's life before God's appointed time.

---

[13] Wikipedia

[14] World Health Organisation WHO report

[15] World Health Organisation WHO report

[16] World Health Organisation WHO report

[17] World Health Organisation WHO report

[18] World Health Organisation WHO report

[19] 2 Peter 3:9

STORIES OF DEATH TRAPS

Many years ago, I was with a friend who was telling me how much he admired my life. He said he wished that he was as committed to God as I was (and still am) and that he was sure that when I died, I would go to Heaven. He expressed a willingness to sit down with me one day so I could show him how I did it by looking through the Bible. I agreed that we should do that some time. At the time, he and some friends were en route to a party and had come over to pick up my older brother.

A few days later, a riot broke out outside my friend's house. He heard the commotion outside but remained in his sitting room, looking outside. We never got to have that talk because on the day of that riot, a stray bullet from an anti-riot policeman found its way into my friend's sitting room and straight into his forehead.

Recently, I heard another story of a man who was overjoyed at how God had saved his life. He gave a testimony in France about how his life was spared during an ambush attack. In less than 24 hours after the testimony, he boarded a flight to Lagos, Nigeria and then from there onto Abuja, Nigeria where his family stayed. He never made it home because he died in a plane crash on the last leg of his journey.

On July 7, 2005, a young graduate full of promise came out safely from the bombed train in London. He quickly called his father back home in Nigeria to inform him of his narrow escape. He also told his dad that he would be taking a bus instead. He got onto the Bus 30 that got bombed at Tavistock Square. His father could not believe it when he was told his son was dead.

These true stories show that when death has an appointment with one, he relentlessly seeks the person out. Death is very good at keeping appointments.

The Kennedy Curse

Wikipedia clearly documents the evidence of a possible curse over the Kennedy family. It is outlined below.

'The Kennedy-tragedies, colloquially called the Kennedy Curse, is a term sometimes used to describe a series of tragedies involving members of the Kennedy family. Some have called the continual misfortune of the Kennedy family a curse. Several members of the family have died from unnatural causes. Most notably are brothers John and Robert, who were assassinated by gunshots in 1963 and 1968 and John, Jr., who was killed in an airplane crash along with his wife and sister-in-law in 1999.

Believers in the curse generally cite the following core events as evidence of the family's misfortunes:
1941 – Rosemary Kennedy, a younger sister of President Kennedy, was believed to be mentally retarded. However, some sources have claimed she was suffering from mental illness, such as depression. Because of her increasingly violent and severe mood swings, her father, Joseph P. Kennedy, Sr., arranged in secret for her to undergo a lobotomy. The surgery impaired her cognitive abilities further and as a result, she remained institutionalised until her death in 2005.
August 12, 1944 – Joseph P. Kennedy, Jr., the older brother of the later President Kennedy, was killed in action in a mid-air aircraft explosion over eastern England while flying a hazardous mission during World War II.
May 13, 1948 – Kathleen Cavendish, Marchioness of Hartington,

a younger sister of the late President Kennedy, was killed in a plane crash in France along with her ill-fated companion, Peter Wentworth-Fitzwilliam, 8th Earl Fitzwilliam.

August 23, 1956 – Jacqueline Bouvier Kennedy, the wife of then future President Kennedy, gave birth to her stillborn daughter, Arabella Kennedy. (Although the daughter was unnamed and was buried at Arlington National Cemetery next to her parents with a marker reading "Daughter", reports later indicated that the Kennedys had intended to name her Arabella.)

August 9, 1963 – Patrick Bouvier Kennedy, son of President Kennedy and First Lady Jacqueline Kennedy, born six weeks premature, died two days after his birth.

November 22, 1963 – U.S. President John F. Kennedy was assassinated by Lee Harvey Oswald, in Dallas, Texas.

June 19, 1964 – U.S. Senator Edward M. "Ted" Kennedy, the youngest brother of the late President Kennedy, was involved in a plane crash in which one of his aides and the pilot were killed. He was pulled from the wreckage by fellow senator Birch E. Bayh II (D-Ind.) and spent weeks in a hospital recovering from a broken back, a punctured lung, broken ribs and internal bleeding.

June 6, 1968 – U.S. Senator Robert F. Kennedy, a younger brother of the late President Kennedy, was assassinated by Sirhan Sirhan in Los Angeles immediately following his victory in the California Democratic presidential primary.

July 18, 1969 – In the Chappaquiddick incident, a car driven by Ted Kennedy goes off a bridge on Martha's Vineyard, eventually drowning his passenger Mary Jo Kopechne. In his July 25 televised statement, Kennedy stated that on the night of the incident he wondered "whether some awful curse did actually hang over all the Kennedys."

August 13, 1973 – Joseph P. Kennedy II, the eldest son of Robert F. Kennedy, was the driver in a car accident that left one passenger, Pam Kelley, permanently paralyzed.

November 17, 1973 – Edward M. Kennedy, Jr., a son of Ted Kennedy, lost a portion of his right leg due to bone cancer at the age of 12.

April 25, 1984 – David Anthony Kennedy, son of Robert F. Kennedy, died from a Demerol and cocaine overdose in a Palm Beach, Florida hotel room.

1991 - William Kennedy Smith, a nephew of President Kennedy, was tried for rape and was acquitted of all charges.

December 31, 1997 – Michael LeMoyne Kennedy, son of Robert F. Kennedy, was killed in a skiing accident in Aspen, Colorado.

July 16, 1999 – John F. Kennedy, Jr., the oldest and only surviving son of President Kennedy, was killed in a plane crash along with his wife and sister-in-law when the Piper Saratoga light aircraft he was piloting crashed into the Atlantic Ocean off the coast of Martha's Vineyard due to pilot error.'

Once again, I ask you to judge – is it mere coincidence that one family has had such a large number of negative and often fatal incidents?

SYMPTOMS AND SIGNS OF PREMATURE DEATH

- There is an impending fear of death in your life that controls your thoughts, decisions and actions.
- There may be evidence of premature death, suicidal thoughts or suicide in your family.
- There may have been an abortion, whether open or secret, in your family.

BREAKING A PREMATURE APPOINTMENT WITH DEATH

In 2 Kings 20:1-7, Hezekiah was sick and near death. He got a message from the prophet Isaiah that he *'should put his house in order because he was going to die and not recover'*. Hezekiah, instead of receiving the prophecy, turned and cried unto God. If it is not your time, it is possible to negotiate with God and stop the enemy's plans in order to live one's life to the fullest. God added 15 more years to Hezekiah's lifespan.

PRAYER POINTS AGAINST THE ASSIGNMENT OF DEATH

Death – Pray against the impending fear of death, premature deaths in your family and suicidal thoughts.

DECLARE

(Insert name) will not die, but live to declare the works of the Lord in the land of the living. I declare that according to the Word of God in Psalm 91:16 (Insert name) will be satisfied with long life and know His salvation. I declare that abundant life is (Insert name) - John 10:10. I cancel every satanic appointment with death in Jesus name. I say deadly assailants and demonic agents of death will not find (Insert name) in Jesus name. Long life is (Insert name) portion, wellbeing and health is (Insert name) portion. I will see my children's children and declare the goodness of the Lord in my generation. I declare you will carry (Insert name) into old age and even in old age (Insert name) .shall be fresh and flourishing in Jesus name.

Pray this as often as necessary when anxious of impending death and make up your own using the following scriptures.

Psalm 118:17
I shall not die, but live and declare the works of the LORD.

Psalm 91:16
With long life I will satisfy him and show him My salvation.

Psalm 116:8-9
For You have delivered my soul from death, my eyes from tears, *and* my feet from falling. I will walk before the LORD In the land of the living.

Ezekiel 18:28
Because he considers and turns away from all the transgressions which he committed, he **shall** surely **live**; he **shall not die**.

Exodus 9:4
And the LORD will make a difference between the **live**stock of Israel and the **live**stock of Egypt. So **not**hing **shall die** of all that belongs to the children of Israel.

Ezekiel 18:17
Who has withdrawn his hand from the poor and **not** received usury or increase, but has executed My judgments and walked in My statutes — He **shall not die** for the iniquity of his father; He **shall** surely **live**!

Isaiah 65:20
No more **shall** an infant from there **live** but a few days, nor an old man who has **not** fulfilled his days; for the child **shall die** one hundred years old.

John 10:10

I have come that they may have **life** and that they may have it more **abundant**ly.

Psalm 92:14

They shall still bear fruit in **old age**; They shall be fresh and flourishing.

Isaiah 46:4

Even to your **old age**, I am He and even to gray hairs I will carry you! I have made and I will bear; even I will carry and will deliver you.

CHAPTER TWO

DISEASE

WHAT IS A DISEASE?

According to *Wikipedia*, a disease is an abnormal condition affecting the body of an organism. It is often construed to be a medical condition associated with specific symptoms and signs may be caused by external factors, such as infectious disease, or it may be caused by internal dysfunctions, such as autoimmune diseases. Ecologically, disease is defined as the maladjustment of the body with the environment. In humans, "disease" is often used more broadly to refer to any condition that causes pain, dysfunction, distress, social problems and/or death to the person afflicted, or similar problems for those in contact with the person. In this broader sense, it sometimes includes injuries, disabilities, disorders, syndromes, infections. A diseased body is quite often not only because of some dysfunction of a particular organ but can also be because of a state of mind of the affected person.

THE FACTS

- UNAIDS and the WHO estimate that AIDS has 25 million people since it was first recognized i.   ...ng it one of the most destructive pandemics[11].
- Obesity is the leading preventable cause of death worldwide[12].
- South Africa has the largest number of HIV patients in the world followed by Nigeria.[13]
- According to WHO, more than 30% of cancer could be prevented by modifying   or avoiding key risk factors, 25% of deaths in the U.S are caused by heart diseases[14].

If the enemy cannot kill you (which is his ultimate plan), he will try to maim or impair your faculties in order to greatly compromise the quality of your life. The aim is so that, even though you are alive, you are unable to live life to the fullest.

'Satan comes to steal, kill and destroy ...' He does some of his destroying through diseases.

BIBLICAL EXAMPLES

The woman with the spirit of infirmity, in Luke 13:11, was so ill she was bent over. Although she was alive, the disease which was the culprit here ensured that she was crippled and maimed for 18 years of her life. Eighteen years equates to about a quarter of an average life. Those years of her life were stolen; her quality of life was

---

[21] Wikipedia

[22] World Health Organisation WHO report

[23] Wikipedia

[24] World Health Organisation WHO report

[25] John 10:10

significantly diminished. She would not have been able to work or look after herself. She would have been totally dependent on others who may or may not have been sympathetic.

The woman with the issue of blood would not have been able to have children and therefore not known the joy of mothering.

The Bible also speaks of those whose lives were blighted with leprosy.[15] Lepers were socially excluded and so lived a life away from regular people. They were hidden away, always covered, could not be gainfully employed and therefore were not self-sufficient. Disease stole away a full life from them.

The Bible also mentions blind men[16] who would never have been able to see their wives, children or appreciate the beauty of nature and life.

For some of these people, death may have been better option.

CONTEMPORARY INFIRMITIES

Most diseased people today are not blind or lepers; but rather they are infiltrated with the diseases prevalent in our society nowadays. Many of them are inherited, stress-related or lifestyle diseases such as hypertension, heart diseases, arthritis, cancer, diabetes, HIV and AIDS.

Each of these diseases greatly compromises the quality of one's life. Many of these diseases affect eating habits, relationships, leisure and eventually lifespan. Affected people may also have to deal with barrenness (physical, spiritually or emotionally) – which is the whole point of the disease – to affect the ability to produce or reproduce.

While some diseases are caused by a demon, many are not. Diseases are often caused by poor lifestyle choices and stresses such as sexual immorality, smoking and lack of exercise.

Some diseases are inherited or familial and some are psycho-somatic diseases which are caused by ailments of the mind such as anger, unforgiveness, worry, anxiety and bitterness. These mind behaviours can also open the door to the enemy which cause further damage. Once they have a foothold within the individual, they can become perpetuated within the family line.

THE HEALTH CONSEQUENCES OF SIN

...*There is* no health in my bones because of my sin. For my iniquities have gone over my head; like a heavy burden they are too heavy for me. Psalm 38:3-4.

Many common diseases such as HIV and other sexually transmitted diseases are often the result of a promiscuous and sinful lifestyle. Ancillary acts such as abortion or barrenness that can be a result of such activity produces feelings of guilt and condemnation which can further exacerbate health complications. Other things such as the subterfuge and lying involved in for example conducting an adulterous affair, fraud or other illicit activity are also highly

---

[26] Leviticus 13

[27] Leviticus 19:14

stressful and reverse wellbeing. It is important to know that sin is destructive spiritually and physically and the wise person who will live long and well is one who avoids sin.

Do not be wise in your own eyes; Fear the LORD and depart from evil.   It will be health to your flesh and strength to your bones. Proverbs 3:7-9

DO NOT KILL THE HORSE YOU RIDE ON

I believe God has given every person (Minister) a message and a "horse" (body) to ride on to deliver the message within a specific time frame. If we are negligent in the care of our "horse" and we die we will never fully deliver our message (fulfil our potential).

As a qualified Medical Doctor, I was able to gently encourage three of my Ministry colleagues to go for a medical check-up. One of them died a few years later and the other two were discovered to have dangerously high levels of cholesterol in the blood while one of them was said to be diabetic. Both of these men diagnosed with these high risk diseases are two of the most anointed men I know personally. Another lovely Pastor colleague of mine collapsed just after leading a prayer meeting and died soon after from a hypertensive disorder. The following 8 out of 12 Healing Evangelists written about by Roberts Liardon in his book 'God's Generals' had this unfortunate twist to their stories:

- Alexander Dowie suffered a debilitating stroke, was confined to a wheelchair for many years and later died.
- Maria Woodworth Ether lost 5 of 6 children to illness.

- Evan Roberts suffered physical and emotional collapse.
- William Seymour died of heart failure at age 52.
- John G. Lake's wife died of physical exhaustion.
- Amie Simple-Mcpherson died of amoebic dysentery at 54.
- Jack Coe died from exhaustion and polio at age 39.
- A.A Allen died with high levels of alcohol in his blood.

I included the above so that you do not believe the myth that if you only take care of God's ministry He will take care of your health. You need to be a good steward of your body even though we know God can heal any disease. We need to take good care of our bodies - taking time to eat healthy and nutritious food, to work out/exercise, get rest and sleep well. Unfortunately, the records show that many of us are not taking such good care of ourselves. Many are overweight and unfit.

WHAT ARE COMMON HEALTH CONSEQUENCES OF BEING OVERWEIGHT AND OBESE?

According to *Wikipedia*, being overweight and obese lead to serious health consequences. Risk increases progressively as BMI increases. Raised body mass index (BMI) is a major risk factor for chronic diseases such as:

- Cardiovascular disease (mainly heart disease and stroke) - already the world's number one cause of death, killing 17 million people each year.
- Diabetes has rapidly become a global epidemic. WHO projects that death from diabetes will increase by more than 50% worldwide in the next 10 years.

- Musculoskeletal disorders – especially osteoarthritis.
- Some cancers (endometrial, breast and colon).
- Childhood obesity is associated with a higher chance of premature death and disability in adulthood.

According to WHO[17], more than 30% of cancer can be prevented by modifying or avoiding key risk factors, based on a 2005 study by international cancer collaborators. Risk factors include:

- tobacco use
- being overweight or obese
- low fruit and vegetable intake
- physical inactivity
- alcohol use
- sexually transmitted HIV-infection
- urban air pollution
- indoor smoke from household use of solid fuels.

Wisdom for Winning the War against Disease

- Ensure you have regular medical health-checks like annual breast scans, smear tests and prostate health examinations.
- Live a sin-free life in order not to give a foothold to the enemy.
- Have a stress-free and worry-free lifestyle by not smoking, getting plenty of exercise and forming healthy eating habits and getting adequate rest.
- Live a life of prayer – believe and speak the Word of God over your life regularly.

---

[28] World Health Organisation WHO report

Prayer Points against the Assignment of Disease

Jesus, thank You that You sent Your Word and healed my disease. I thank You that wholeness and total wellbeing is my lot with You (John 10:10) – disease and sickness shall not have dominion over me in Jesus name. Lord Jesus put Your hand on me and cause every sickness in my body to disappear (Luke 13:13). I thank You that You became a curse for me and bore all my infirmities so that I would not have to (Galatians 3:13); therefore I declare (insert the name of the disease e.g. cancer, barrenness, low sperm count) is not my portion. I lay hold of the fullness of life in You. I gain wisdom to be healthy and power to overcome disease in Jesus name; I declare it is well with me, in Jesus name. Amen.

Matthew 10:1

'And when He had called His twelve disciples to Him, He gave them power over unclean spirits, to cast them out and to heal all kinds of sickness and all kinds of disease'. There is power to deal with every kind of disease. Pray against any debilitating or terminal disease e.g. cancer, HIV, diabetes, hypertension, barrenness as these ailments are not our portion as children of the most high. Use the scriptures below to declare and secure your healing.

Luke 13: 12 -13

But when Jesus saw her, He called her to Him and said to her, "woman, you are loosed from your infirmity." 13 And He laid His hands on her and immediately she was made straight and glorified God.

Exodus 23:25

"So you shall serve the LORD your God and He will bless your bread and your water. And I will take **sickness** away from the midst of you.

Deuteronomy 7:15

And the LORD will take away from you all **sickness** and will afflict you with none of the terrible diseases of Egypt which you have known, but will lay them on all those who hate you.

Matthew 4:23

And Jesus went about all Galilee, teaching in their synagogues, preaching the gospel of the kingdom and healing all kinds of **sickness** and all kinds of disease among the people.

Matthew 8:17

that it might be fulfilled which was spoken by Isaiah the prophet, saying: "He Himself took our infirmities and bore our **sickness**es."

CHAPTER THREE

DEBT (POVERTY)

WHAT IS DEBT?

A debt is something that is owed or that one is bound to pay to or perform for another. It is a liability or obligation to pay or render something. It is the condition of being under such an obligation with the accruing of further debt in the form of interest if the original debt is not paid on time.

It could be an offence requiring reparation; a sin; a trespass.

The Facts[18]
- Average household debt in the UK is £8,985 excluding mortgages.
- The average household debt in the UK is £59,670 including mortgage.
- One person in the UK is declared insolvent every 4.8 minutes.
- In the UK around 124 properties are repossessed everyday.
- The amount of interest paid on debt in the UK has now reached

£252 million a day.

- Approximately 25% of people in debt in the UK are finding it difficult to cope and doctors say that the depression and anxiety due to debt is very common.
- More than 8 million people around the world die every year due to extreme poverty related causes.

What is Poverty?

Many are poor even in the developed world. Poverty is the state or condition of having little or no money, goods, or means of support. It is also the deficiency of necessary or desirable ingredients and qualities. It is a state of deprivation and lack of necessities. Poverty denotes a serious lack of the means for proper existence. Extreme poverty or destitution implies a state of having absolutely none of the necessities of life.

Poverty is therefore a condition where a person is deprived of or lacks the essentials for a minimum standard of living or well being. Economists have a measuring stick which they use to measure poverty known as the "Poverty line". It is the minimum level of income deemed necessary to achieve an adequate standard of living.

How poor are you?

Poverty cannot be measured by one's level of income or earning capacity alone, but should be measured by the amount a person has leftover to survive on after the individual's debts and liabilities have been paid.

---

[29] http://www.creditaction.org.uk/debt-statistics/2010/august-2010.html

Poverty is relative

If we were to go by the former definition, only those who are unemployed or those who earn below the minimum wage will be considered poor, but by the latter definition many more people can be deemed to be poor as a result of massive liabilities or as a consequence of their accumulated debt.

Wherever you see Poverty, Greed is always nearby

This holds true whether in the degenerate back streets of the slums of Africa or in the tower blocks in the council estates of inner city London.

In the developing nations, the unequal distribution of wealth may be due to some corrupt leaders who have diverted public funds or donations made by international relief agencies into his personal Swiss bank account. In the developing world, unequal distribution of wealth is more likely to be due to the activities of greedy bankers who give a large mortgage loan or credit card at cut throat interest rates, to people who will be significantly worse off as a result. These are two different methods but both are designed to keep the masses poor and a few very rich.

This is not to put the blame for poverty squarely on the shoulders of the rich, but to underscore the fact that many causes of poverty are systemic.

A Modern form of Slavery

In the western world there is a subtle but definite system designed to keep people in debt, so that they can continue to pay interest.

It is the same kind of system that was evident in the time of Nehemiah as seen in the text below.

"1Now there arose a great cry of the [poor] people and of their wives [driven to borrowing] against their Jewish brethren [the few who could afford to lend].

2For some said, we, our sons and daughters, are many; therefore allow us to take grain that we may eat and live! If we are not given grain, let us take it!

3Also some said, we are mortgaging our lands, vineyards and houses to buy grain because of the scarcity.

4Others said, we have borrowed money on our fields and vineyards to pay the [Persian] king's heavy tax.

5Although our flesh is the same as that of our brethren and our children are as theirs, yet we are forced to sell our children as slaves; some of our daughters have already been thus sold and we are powerless to redeem them, for others have our lands and vineyards.

6I [Nehemiah] was very angry when I heard their cry and these words.

7I thought it over and then rebuked the nobles and officials. I told them, you are exacting interest from your own kinsmen. And I held a great assembly against them.

⁸I said to them, we, according to our ability, have bought back our Jewish brethren who were sold to the nations; but will you even sell your brethren, that they may be sold to us? Then they were silent and found not a word to say.

⁹Also I said, what you are doing is not good. Should you not walk in the fear of our God to prevent the taunts and reproach of the nations, our enemies?

¹⁰I, my brethren and my servants are lending them money and grain. Let us <u>stop this forbidden interest</u>

¹¹Return this very day to them their fields, vineyards, olive groves and houses and also a hundredth of all the money, grain, new wine and oil that you have exacted from them.

¹²Then they said, we will restore these and require nothing from them. We will do as you say. Then I called the priests and took an oath of the lenders that they would do according to this promise" (Amplified Nehemiah1:1-12).

THE SYSTEM OF DEBT

The system then was so bad that the borrowers had to mortgage not only their lands, vineyards and houses in order to buy food but they also sold their daughters into slavery (possibly forced prostitution).

"The rich <u>rules</u> over the poor and the borrower is <u>servant</u> to the lender" Proverbs 22:7.

A similar system is operative today, where bankers lure unsuspecting customers with the bait of attractive bank, student, house improvement and car loans, store and credit cards, payday loans and mortgages with sometimes astronomical interest rates on the loans that make it almost impossible for them to pay back in a lifetime.

I Owe! I Owe! I Owe! Off to Work I go

This system is so pervasive that most people in the western world are living under a massive debt burden they will never fully pay. For many, almost everything they own was bought on credit hence they are paying for yesterday's luxuries with money that should be for today's necessities. This leaves them with little or nothing to survive on. With the average household debt in the UK at £59,670 (including mortgage), it would mean that the entire future working life of the average man or woman in the U.K goes primarily towards paying debts.

The Effects of Debt on People

Although debt creeps in subtly and quietly, when it gets into a person's life and home it becomes so oppressive that it leads to stress, sleeplessness, shame, limitation, marital conflict and in many cases eventually leads to divorce.

"Let my people go"

When God saw the injustice of slavery which the Egyptians

enforced upon Israel, He sent Moses to emancipate His people from the intense oppression. Moses was sent by God to liberate the Jews specifically so that they could serve Him with their time and worship Him with their treasure as seen in the following scriptures.

"And the LORD spoke to Moses, "Go to Pharaoh and say to him, 'Thus says the LORD: "Let My people go, that they may <u>serve Me</u> (Time)" (Exodus 8:1).

"Then Pharaoh called for Moses and Aaron and said, "Entreat the LORD that He may take away the frogs from me and from my people; and I will let the people go, that they may <u>sacrifice to the LORD</u> (Treasure)" (Exodus 8:8).

We then see in the verses that follow that despite God's judgments through Moses, the enemy drove a very hard bargain. Even when he was really pushed to the wall he still wanted to withhold the Israelites wealth and their **children**.

This remains the enemy's ploy till today; if he cannot keep you out of certain privileges and a future eternity with God, he will make every attempt to keep you in debt so you never have enough time or treasure to serve God and build His Kingdom thus ensuring that you continue to perpetuate a spirit of debt in order to keep your children in bondage.

"And Pharaoh said, "I will let you go, that you may sacrifice to the LORD your God in the wilderness; only you shall not go very far away. Intercede for me."
"8 So Moses and Aaron were brought again to Pharaoh and he said to them, "Go, serve the LORD your God. Who are the ones that are going?"
9 And Moses said, "We will go with <u>our young</u> and our old; with

our sons and our daughters, with our flocks and our herds we will go, for we must hold a feast to the LORD."

10 Then he said to them, "The LORD had better be with you when I let you and your little ones go! Beware, for evil is ahead of you.

11 "Not so! Go now, you who are men and serve the LORD, for that is what you desired." And they were driven out from Pharaoh's presence.

12 Then the LORD said to Moses, "Stretch out your hand over the land of Egypt for the locusts, that they may come upon the land of Egypt and eat every herb of the land-all that the hail has left" *(Exodus10:8-12).*

Debt is a Spirit

Debt is a spirit or an attitude that can be perpetuated from one generation to another. People get into debt for a variety of reasons such as covetousness, greed, selfishness, indulgence, laziness, lack of discipline or ignorance. Essentially we fall into a cycle of debt when we become "Slaves of Pleasure".

Dennis Kimbro in his book, '*Think and Grow Rich, A Black Choice*', encourages people of colour to move from a consumer to an investment Mentality. He emphasises that we have become slaves to our pleasures by showing that:

- 36% of Hair care products are bought by people of colour.
- 30% of Movie theatre tickets are bought by people of colour.
- 28% of GQ magazine are bought by people of colour.
- 20% of portable TV products are bought by people of colour.
- People of colour spend $6 billion on Coca Cola and $500,000 on Mc Donald's annually.

Small wonder we have remained in a perpetual cycle of debt.

WE CAN REALLY MAKE POVERTY HISTORY[19]

Up to half of Africa's population live on less than 1 dollar a day. Of the 49 least developed countries described as the poorest in the world, 37 are Africans.

The world's richest 225 people have a combined income equal to the annual income of almost half the worlds' poorest.

If the world is really serious about making poverty history, the rich can help liberate the poor through their generous giving, training and more importantly reducing the interest charged on monies borrowed.

HOW CAN YOU GET OUT OF DEBT?

I teach a full seminar of how you can break out of debt, but in this book, I will give a quick snapshot.

1. Change your mindset by moving from a consumer to an investment mentality.

2. Planning

Only 8 of the 12 months income you worked for is yours. If you don't plan what you spend, your money will go where you never

---

[30] Peter Meadows, (2003) The Rich thinking about the Worlds poor, Authentic Lifestyle

sent it. A Budget defends your priorities from casual wishes and impulsive spending.

3. Saving (Keep something back)

Save 10-20% of your income by living on 80% of what you earn. If you save £10 for 30 days at 10% compound interest, it will yield £125,000 in 15 years and £1,900,000 in 40 years.

4. Discipline (Don't Spend all you earn)

Do not increase your appetite when your income increases. Live below your means.

5. Prudence (Spend less when you buy)

Shop at sales, One pound shops and car boot sales.

6. Faithfulness (Managing and Accountable)

Handle small things like the big things e.g. by keeping records so you know where your money goes.

"Be diligent to know the state of your flocks and attend to your herds; 24 For riches are not forever, Nor does a crown endure to all generations. 26 The lambs will provide your clothing and the goats the price of a field; 27 You shall have enough goats' milk for your food, For the food of your household and the nourishment of your maidservants" (Proverbs 27:23-27).

7. Wisdom (e.g. Debt management, Tax Efficiency)

Get wisdom on money management and wealth creation. Read books and attend seminars on the subjects.

8. Knowledge (Assets or Liabilities)

Aim to move from liabilities (things that take money from you such as loans) to owning assets. An asset is anything that puts money into your pocket such as dividends from stocks, rent from a property or income that does not have to be put toward paying off liabilities.

9. Selling (Sell on eBay)

Sell old stuff to buy new items or to buy assets e.g. a business or property.

10. Timing (Patience)/ Delayed Gratification

Get into the habit of waiting to have things. Instead of buying things on credit, save up and pay cash instead.

11. Start a Business

Identify your gifts and start a business around it that puts some extra money in your pocket.

"Prepare your outside work, Make it fit for yourself in the field; and afterward build your house" (Proverbs 24:27).

12. Break the Spirit of Debt in Prayer

PRAYER POINTS AGAINST THE ASSIGNMENT OF DEBT

Debt – Pray against poverty, lack, wastefulness, debt, bankruptcy and ask for the grace to give.

PRAYER

I break the stronghold of debt over my life and declare according to the Word of God that I will be a lender and not a borrower **(Deuteronomy 15:6)**. I thank God for divine assistance to clear debt like the prophet's widow (2 Kings 4:6-8). I rebuke every devourer in my life **(Malachi 3:10-11)** and declare that I am not wasteful or extravagant. Right now I receive a diligent and resourceful spirit. I receive wisdom to manage my resources wisely. Father I thank you for the power to create wealth **(Deuteronomy 8:18)**.I declare I will spot opportunities and will sow at the right time that I may reap at the right time **(Proverbs 20:4)**. I declare I will always have to give to those in need **(2 Corinthians 9:8).**

Scriptures for prayer

Malachi 3:10-11
Bring all the tithes into the storehouse, That there may be food in My house and try Me now in this," Says the LORD of hosts, "If I will not open for you the windows of heaven and pour out for you such blessing That there will not be room enough to receive it. 11 "And I will rebuke the devourer for your sakes,"

2 Corinthians 9:8
And God is able to make all grace abound toward you, that you, always having all sufficiency in all things, may have abundance for every good work.

John 6:13
Therefore they **gathered** them up and filled twelve baskets with the fragments of the five barley **loaves** which were left over by those who had eaten.

Deuteronomy 15:6
For the LORD your God will bless you just as He promised you; you shall **lend** to many nations, but you shall **not borrow**; you shall reign over many nations, but they shall **not** reign over you.
Deuteronomy 28:12

The LORD will open to you His good treasure, the heavens, to give the rain to your land in its season and to bless all the work of your hand. You shall **lend** to many nations, but you shall **not borrow**.

Philippians 4:19
And my God shall **supply** all your **need** according to His riches in glory by Christ Jesus.

Psalm 37:25
I have been young and now am old; yet I have not seen the **righteous forsaken**, nor his descendants **begging bread**.

Deuteronomy 8:18
And you shall remember the LORD your God, for it is He who gives you **power** to get **wealth**, that He may establish His covenant which He swore to your fathers, as it is this day.

2 Kings 4:6-8
Then she came and told the man of God. And he said, "Go, sell the oil and **pay your debt**; and you and **your** sons live on the rest."

Philippians 4:11-13
I know how to be **abase**d and I know how to **abound**. Everywhere and in all things I have learned both to be full and to be hungry, both to **abound** and to suffer need.

Proverbs 10:5
He who gathers in summer is a wise son; He who sleeps in **harvest** is a son who causes shame.)

Proverbs 20:4
The lazy man will not plow because of winter; He will beg during **harvest** and have nothing.

Psalm 107:37
And sow fields and plant vineyards, that they may yield a fruitful **harvest**.

He also blesses them and they multiply greatly; And He does not let their cattle decrease.

SECTION 2

FAMILY TERRORISERS

CHAPTER FOUR

DEFILEMENT (SEXUAL IMMORALITY)

The Facts

- 44% of parishioners confessed they have visited pornographic websites in the last one year[20]
- America spends $10 billion dollars on pornography every year – the same amount it spends on foreign aid [21]
- 33% of Pastors confess "inappropriate" sexual behaviour with someone in the church[22]
- 20% of Pastors admitted to having an affair while in ministry[23]

These statistics demonstrate that the devil is hard at work in this area.

EXTRA MARITAL SEXUAL ACTIVITY

"Marriage is honourable among all and the bed undefiled; but fornicators and adulterers God will judge" (Hebrew 11:3).

2 out of every 3 non Christian married men have had affairs outside marriage. For the women, it is 1 out of every 3; 30% have had affairs they could admit to. According to *Christianity Today,* 23% of Christian couples admit to extra-marital sex and improprieties; that is not counting those who would not come clean.

Much more alarming is the empirical revelation that 12% of Pastors confessed that they had engaged in sexual intercourse with someone other than their spouses, that is, they had extra-marital affairs. Candidly speaking, I don't know about you or your standards but I think 12% is a lot! In fact, 2% is a lot! 12% is over a tithe of Pastors and a tithe is representative of the whole. These survey figures only categorise people who volunteered their confessions to inappropriate sexual behaviour or "submitted" to the statistical scope.

Within the Church, available statistics evidently underscore the fact that the Church is already infected with the same disease that the world is suffering. This infection is no respecter of persons indeed. It has affected both the parishioners and the priests, leaving no one out.

PREMARITAL SEXUAL ACTIVITY

In 1991, a study by Professor Francis and Dr. Kane[24], which targeted teenagers as the major subjects, unveiled very alarming

---

[31] London, H.B. Jr., (2003) Pastors at Greater Risk, Gospel Light Publications

[32] Williams, Jessica, (2007) 50 facts that should change the world, Icon Books

[33] London, H.B. Jr., (2003) Pastors at Greater Risk, Gospel Light Publications

[34] London, H.B. Jr., (2003) Pastors at Greater Risk, Gospel Light Publications

statistics. 41% of the young people interviewed claimed to have had sex before age 16. Though age 16 is supposedly the age of consent in the United Kingdom, many are apparently flouting it. By age 20, 88% were sexually active. This study was carried out in 1991and I can assure you that it is much worse now.

Another survey conducted in 1991 by *Mac Europe and Agape UK*[25] to observe teenage sexual tendencies and attitudes in the Church records that 31% within the 13 – 16 age range thought sexual intercourse was alright if both partners consented and 20% admitted they were already sexually active. It is unfortunate and disheartening to note that no matter how moderate this percentage seems, 20% of our Christian teenagers are already sexually active! I am often shocked and alarmed by the numbers of teenagers who come up to me for confession and counselling on sex related issues. A particular girl once said "I'm only 14 years old but I just want to tell you that I've had sex already. What should I do?" There is indeed a big problem in today's modern world.

A Canadian magazine published the result of a survey on women's sexuality and their sexual behaviour. The set of statistics revealed that in 1966, 69% had sex before marriage and by the '80s that number increased to 90%. I leave what the statistics might be today to your imagination.

The figures on premarital sexual activity in Christendom and the world are, in my estimation, too close for comfort. Each time I look back at some of the premarital guidance sessions my wife and I have conducted over the years, I have deduced that only about two in every ten couples completely abstain from sex before marriage.

It is a sad commentary that so few believers refrain from sexual intercourse before the Clergy can pronounce them as "man and wife." Why should that be when it is a widely known fact that sex before marriage is unscriptural? Oh God help us!

EXPOSING SEXUAL TRAPS

There is no arguing with the fact that one of the most potent traps of the enemy set against the Church is sexual sin and no one is exempted. Why is sexual sin so prevalent? It is so because the enemy watches, seduces and traps his victims through their minds and emotions. There is a mind battle; an intelligence warfare going on and you must always win in order to live a victorious life.

In the physical, battles are fought and won through the use of surveillance, men, machines and intelligence. In like manner, you can win every battle against the enemy if you know what it takes to expose and disarm his subtle traps. Apostle Paul, in 2 Corinthians 2:10-11, warns that we, New Testament Christians, should not be ignorant of the devices or strategies of the devil. This means that the devil is a sinister strategic planner par-excellence! The word - *Strategy* is derived from the word – stratagem which the *Webster Dictionary* defines as 'a manoeuvre, designed to deceive an enemy at war, a scheme of deceit'.

So what are the sexual sins that the enemy has designed to entrap us? They are adultery, fornication, homosexuality, pornography and masturbation to say the least. Immoral acts and sexual sins are so prevalent today because Satan studies, sets up and seduces his victims into sexual entrapment. You will not be trapped. Read on as we discover how the enemy entraps his preys.

---

[35] Professor Francis and Dr. Kane

[36] Marc Europe and Agape UK

Infidelity

According to Dr. Linda Mintle in her book, "*Divorce proofing your Marriage*", infidelity can be defined as a breach of trust, a breaking of the marriage covenant or a betrayal of the relationship. It goes beyond sexual intercourse to include the physical, emotional and thought life of a person.

Mintle says, infidelity requires meeting a need outside the boundary of your covenant. If a person finds someone other than their spouse attractive, they have a choice – to act on it or turn away. The enemy works hard at enticing people into inappropriate behaviour.

Ecclesiastes 7:26 says 'And I find more bitter than death the **woman** whose heart is **snare**s and nets, whose hands are fetters. He who pleases God shall escape from her, but the sinner shall be trapped by her'. This scripture makes it clear that some people have an evil agenda - to ensnare others; and when we do not choose what is right, we open the door for the enemy to have dominion through sin. Once we choose to gratify our ungodly desires, we are in enemy territory. Of course it doesn't stop there, Dr Mintle points out that **adultery is not the only sin when one cheats; it opens the door to other sins such as lying. Oftentimes, other fraudulent behaviour begins.**

Below, we will examine the common causes for divorce for women and men in order to determine how the enemy gains entrance into our lives.

Women and Infidelity

According to Dr. Willard F. Harley, Jr.,[26] women tend to be more concerned about their marriages than men. They buy most of the books on marriage in an attempt to improve their marriages and initiate most marriage counselling. They often complain about their marriages to their closest friends and sometimes to anyone who will listen. They also file for divorce twice as often as men!

Why do women seem so dissatisfied with marriage? What do they want from their husbands? What bothers them so much about marriage that some are willing to risk their families' future for it? The reason might be in two of the most frequent reasons given for divorce - mental cruelty and neglect. Surprisingly, few women divorce because of physical abuse, infidelity, alcoholism, criminal behaviour, fraud, or other serious grounds. In fact, I find myself bewildered by women in serious physical danger who refuse to leave men that threaten their safety. Neglect and mental cruelty covers both emotional and physical abandonment. Husbands that work away from the home, leaving their wives alone for weeks at a time, may find they are unwittingly guilty of this.

WHAT MAKES WOMEN MORE PRONE TO EMOTIONAL AFFAIRS?
(A Lady's viewpoint)

You might have watched Tyler Perry's movie titled, "Why Did I Get Married?" Remember the discussion on the 80/20 rule which states that: in a marriage, you will only get 80% of your needs met? An outsider may offer the other 20% and sometimes, a woman wants that 20% so badly that she will gravitate towards the man that is providing it, even if she is not aware of it. That 20%

---

[37] Willard Harley Jr., Women and Infidelity, (article)

represents her margin of vulnerability. However, if a woman reaches for the 20% in someone else, she risks losing out on the 80% that she had; ending up with a whole lot less.

The 20% gap for a woman could be various things. If a woman feels her husband is not a good provider, then a well-earning colleague or boss who provides well for his family may be a temptation. If a woman desires a spiritual head, then the head of the Married Men's Fellowship may be attractive to her. Also, if a woman craves more communication from her husband, then the man that takes time to share and talk to her will be enticing. Some women may be more vulnerable to an ex-partner, especially if they feel they made the wrong choice in a marriage partner. The history between them makes interaction easy and can predispose them to an emotional affair at the very least. Many people still think that an emotional affair is not really adultery. Even when such affairs start to get physical, once there's no intercourse, people still think it's not adultery. Even Bill Clinton said he "did not have sexual relations with that woman" (whom he had had oral sex with)!

Logic, statistics, reason and plain common sense suggest that an emotional affair will become a full-blown affair but many delude themselves that it will not. They think, "I just enjoy talking to him, I just like his counsel, I just like encouraging him, he just encourages me, he says nice things, he asks about my children, my parents, my work, my ministry, my husband!!! Hey, he even prays with me!" This is how the enemy subtly reels us in and before we know it we are on the dangerous and slippery road that many times eventually leads to a full-blown sexual affair.

THE CYCLE OF DISSATISFACTION

Human beings are complex and unique creations. We are created to be attractive and to notice what is attractive. Every single person on the face of the earth is attracted to one type of person or another. Though we all have the seed of attraction planted in us by God we are not supposed to act on every attraction.

When engaged couples come to me for premarital guidance, I always ask one question. I usually ask "Of all the six billion people on the face of the earth, why have you chosen this person?" They usually have a long list of the qualities that the other person has; but the truth is that there are a thousand and one people out there with those same qualities. There will always be someone more handsome, more beautiful or more intelligent than your spouse.

The conclusive point is that although a person can meet a 'better' person than one's spouse, a covenant relationship is one in which a decision is consciously made to love the other person whether that person reciprocates or not and whether that person is loving and lovely or not. Those who do not understand this principle are vulnerable to pre or extra-marital affairs because they are constantly in search of perfection, which is elusive. Before they know it they find themselves between the sheets with someone other than their spouse.

Illicit sex is indeed bondage. Many find themselves lured towards it as they seek for love, satisfaction or significance. They throw caution to the wind despite the destruction they know it'll cause. Why? Because an enemy is at work, operating behind the scene to heighten temptation so that they might succumb and he can gain the platform to frustrate life out of them.

But I believe that God will not leave you at the mercy of your negative habit, being subtly controlled by the evil one. This is your hour of breaking forth. Your season of celebration is here at last.

I see you rising from whatever pit you have been pushed into right now into your great destiny in God. I pray that any habit or temptation that is a challenge to you today will soon come under your control and dominion. In no time from now, you shall look for them but will not find them anymore around you. God will grant you the moral and spiritual courage to go through your journey here on the earth without any stain, strain or pain in Jesus name. Amen.

You can start the journey to victory, by reading, understanding and applying the spiritual truths you are about to encounter into your life. Every object remains at a state of rest until a relevant and equal force is applied to it.

SELF DISCOVERY: THE WAY OUT

As deadly as sexual sin is, God has not left us entirely without a way of escape. To Him, your past is not as important as your future and that bright future starts from the moment you make up your mind to be free. If you have had a negative past due to ignorance and sin, your hour of deliverance can begin today. As you read on, God in His infinite mercies will not only forgive you of your sins but will also open your eyes to those traps and sins that so easily beset you. God is determined to make everything that seems like a challenge to you today become your testimonies tomorrow.

Blessed is she that believeth for there shall be a performance of what the mouth of the Lord has spoken. (Luke 1:45)

The scriptural way of escape is by exposing and avoiding the enemy's traps! The Webster dictionary defines *a trap* as a device for catching unsuspecting animals (notice the emphasis on animals!). It captures or kills, when the victim falls for the bait attached to it. Obviously, a trap is not complete if there are no baits involved. For every trap, there must be bait and that in this context is equivalent to what the victim needs, wants or desires.

The devil's bait is usually disguised as something that appeals to our needs, wants or desires. Without these, it will not be a trap. For instance, to catch a fish, the most likely bait you will use is a worm. There is no point trying to catch a fish by using a wristwatch as bait. The fish would not bite that bait. In like manner, to trap a rabbit, a carrot will be most appropriate. There is no point trying to catch a rabbit with filet mignon because rabbits are not carnivores; they do not eat meat.

In order to avoid or overcome sexual traps, we must first understand our self, our composition and our makeup. It is not until this is done that we can truly hope to fight and overcome the devil, how he works and what his *modus operandi* is. In other words, you must know yourself, your weapons and your strategies in order to forcefully confront and then counter the devil's devices.

There is also no gainsaying the need to understand who you are and what makes you tick. King David demonstrated this in Psalm 139:14 when he said *'I will praise you, for I am fearfully and wonderfully made...'* You need to know your makeup and human constitution very well for in you lies the key to your victory over sexual traps.

Blessed is the man that endureth temptation: for when he is tried, he shall receive the crown of life, which the Lord hath promised to them that love him. Let no man say when he is tempted, I am tempted of God: for God cannot be tempted with evil, neither tempteth he any man: But every man is tempted, when he is drawn away of his own lust and enticed. Then when lust hath conceived, it bringeth forth sin: and sin, when it is finished, bringeth forth death. (James1: 12-15)

Every man is open to the devil's attempts, but the question of yielding to temptation is a matter of choice. God does not tempt and cannot be blamed for any form of temptation you are in at the moment. So, those who resist and overcome sexual temptations or obstinately refuse to be caught by sexual traps are not lucky or more favoured by God than you are.

The truth is that you need to make more effort to put your body under your control and not otherwise. The act of making excuses for your misfortune or weakness is a defeatist theory and it is only when you overcome excuses that you begin to see victory.

Most people caught in sexual traps are fond of claiming that the devil made them do it. The enemy sets the bait, but a person must decide to bite it. Your flesh is always getting ready to lead you astray.

James 1:14 emphasises an undeniable truth that '*every man is tempted*'. Every individual falls within this category so everyone is certainly a candidate for temptation. Again, I remind you that you do not have to fall. The same verse further tightens the noose on human excuses with some deep revelations. It says we are herded down the spiritual self-destruct lane by our own lusts! No divine encouragement there whatsoever.

Every single animal has its own propensities, proclivities, predilections, leanings and inclinations. There is a craving on the inside of every animal including mankind. Each person has a particular weak spot or what you may call an 'Achilles heel'. The devil knows you and he knows your weak spot.

Do you know what that is? Everyone who will overcome must know his/her weakness in order to develop an effective strategy for his or her survival.

THE WHITE SEPULCHRE

Do not be fooled by people's outward appearance. Even the devil often disguises himself as an angel of light, so be warned. The thresholds of vulnerability to sexual sin differ from person to person. The kind of temptation that would make you fall flat out is not the kind that someone else may be susceptible to.

Another crucial point to note is also found in James 1:14. *'Every man is tempted when…'* Temptations do not occur all the time or at every hour on the clock; it has its timing. There is a specific combination of factors on timing that you need to pay attention to in order to avoid or overcome sexual sin.

Temptations are seasonal strategies aimed at drawing you away from your pursuits in life. Sexual sin in particular is intended to pull you out of the will of God and distract to the extent that you miss your appointment with destiny.

James 1:14 further widen our understanding of how and why sexual sins occur. It states that *'every man is drawn away by his own lust…'* Everyone has lusts made to measure or tailor-made for his or her psyche and it is cut to fit each of us in every strata of our entire personality. Everyone has a peculiar lust with which the enemy can bait or entrap him or her with. One man's meat they say is another man's poison.

Your lust may be triggered by one kind of bait while another kind of bait is what will appeals to your friend. Your brand of temptation may be markedly at odds with mine and you may not be tempted by what tempts me.

The gestation cycle of sin is conception, the action and the resultant destruction. See King David and Bathsheba's example below.

David arose from off his bed and walked upon the roof of the king's house: and from the roof he saw a woman washing herself; and the woman was very beautiful to look upon. And David sent and enquired after the woman. And one said, Is not this Bathsheba, the daughter of Eliam, the wife of Uriah the Hittite? And David sent messengers and took her; and she came in unto him and he lay with her; for she was purified from her uncleanness: and she returned unto her house. And the woman conceived and sent and told David and said, I am with child. (2 Samuel 11:1-5)

David's real troubles started when he first looked and beheld, he then conceived in his heart how pleasant it would be to lay with and have sexual intercourse with Bathsheba.

Be mindful of what you think about and what you allow your mind to process for if you cannot stop the thought, you cannot stop the act. Be careful about what you lay with too - whether it is alcohol or drugs – for you shall reap whatever you sow.

The Combination Lock Principle

When I was much younger and in boarding school, each student had a combination lock. These locks were meant to keep safe each student's very valuable food supplies - milk, sugar and other quick-fix foods - in the specific locker assigned to each individual.

The same is true of our lives. A divine lock from God protects every Christian soul. Once you give your life to Christ Jesus, there is a hedge of protection around you with a combination lock of the Spirit that is completely impermeable to the devil and his surrogates.

Have you not considered my servant Job that there is none like him in the earth, a perfect and an upright man, one that feareth God and eschewed evil? (Job 1:8)

God was so confident in Job that He could not but boast about him and all Satan could say was that God had His hedge of protection around Job, which automatically renders sterile, every salvo fired by the accuser of the brethren.

Subsequently, the life lesson here is this - unless God grants Satan the permission or reveals a part of the combinations to your lock, no tempter can gain access into the life of any believer; baits in any fashion, shape or form notwithstanding. As for unbelievers, their lives are completely open to the devil to roam to and fro as he pleases (see 1 Peter 5:8).

Outside Christ and the salvation provided by Jehovah God through His son, Jesus Christ, unbelievers merely exist to provide fodder for the devil's destructive devices. Unbelievers do not stand a chance against the devil and his fiery sexual baits, darts and weapons.

The key to victory over sexual sin therefore is that true self-empowerment is achieved when an individual comes to the knowledge of Jesus Christ as Lord and Saviour and he/she lives in total submission to Him, His Covenant and His will. Prominent in the will of God is that we all lead a lifestyle of sexual purity and propriety. Sexual proclivities outside the institution of marriage have no place in the Covenant of God. Sex is only permitted within the confines of marriage.

Though the Bible expressly states that the whole world is under the sway of the evil one yet there is no way the enemy can operate in your life except your 'combination' is given to him. However, it is so unfortunate that many, through bad choices or outright disobedience, commit avoidable errors by which they handover their 'combination' to the enemy of their soul.

By a stretch of imagination, it is conceivable that one individual may have 6-3-1 combination, another 5-4-2, yet for another 7-7-7, 6-3-6. There is therefore no one without a peculiar combination.
You must know and guard your combination jealously because the devil will keep tweaking the numbers on your combo-lock till he is able to break the code. It is your job to make sure, through complete yieldedness to God that the devil never succeeds.

PRINCIPLE I: SELF KNOWLEDGE

What are the numbers to your combination lock that God has put in place to protect you and how do they work? The first number points to your own weaknesses and particular lust. The Bible narrowed down the broad spectrum of our weaknesses to lust of the eyes, lust of the flesh and the pride of life (see 1 John 2: 16). Every man is tempted in all these three areas but the degree to which we are individually tempted in each of these three counts differ. Put simply, we are all tempted by money, sex and power.

On one hand, there are some men who are tempted by just about anything in a skirt! They even become restless with libidinal energy surging when they see Scottish men in their kilts. These are people who experience sexual vibes just by watching gold fishes swirl around an aquarium. Sexual stimulations come to them in just about any kind of way.

On the other hand, if you put these same people in a room filled with pounds sterling and ask them to keep vigil over that money, there is no way that you will find a penny, not even a mere five pounds in their pocket when you return to check on them. The reason is simple; money does not entice them.

Yet again, there are other individuals who will not steal money or sleep around but as soon as they have an opportunity to talk about what they have achieved; who they think they are or what they are worth - it is at that point that hell is let loose. They cannot resist chipping in unsolicited information about their accomplishments - 'I do own quite an array of landed assets, huge investments in shares and so-so amount of money in the bank.' There are believers who are quick to flash their cards, make sure you note that their residential address is in the wealthy end of town and reel off the make, model and engine capacity or special marquee of their ride. The pride of life is their issue.

There are yet others who cannot but take what is not theirs. They can resist their passion for sex, can give an exact evaluation of their worth without inflating their ego but when it comes to money, they feel powerless. Some people always steal when any amount of money is kept in their custody.

Please know yourself and be sincere about it. If your weakness is smoking, do not go near cigarette vendors or outlets. If yours is pornography, avoid being alone with a laptop when you feel vulnerable. If alcohol makes you susceptible, why go near a wine bar or pub? Run away from friends that inspire you to drink and totally abstain from whomever, wherever and whatever will make you end up staggering out of a place singing the drunkard's signature hiccup sounds.

People vulnerable to drug addiction should absolutely avoid passing through drug red zones like Kings Cross in London. If gossip has you in its grasp, avoid long telephone conversations without a purpose or anything that can act as a catalyst for setting you off on that tangent of sin. Are you a glutton for food? Then keep your fridge bare except for the essentials and avoid eating between meals. The big picture is this: know your own lust and avoid the places, people and circumstances that make you vulnerable.

PRINCIPLE II: TIMING

You must not only know your weaknesses but also the most probable time that temptations will come.

To everything there is a season, a time for every purpose under heaven: A time to be born and a time to die, a time to plant and a time to pluck out what is planted. (Ecclesiastes 3:1)

The second principle and combination in the lock is what you might call vulnerable moments or occasions. Do you know your 'when? 'There is a lust in you that comes to the fore in certain seasons. Some women become sexually uncontrollable around and during their ovulation cycle. In others, it could be a change in temperament around their menstrual cycle that triggers their weaknesses.

For some men, their appetite for sex is fully awake in summer when temperatures are sizzling and ladies dress scantily. For these men, summer makes everything visible.

For a lot of single women, winter makes them vulnerable, weak and wanton. For instance, a particular young lady I use to know said on one October day a few years ago that she had to find a husband because she desperately needed a man to warm her bed during winter. I felt like telling her that what she needed was not a bed mate but an electrically warmed duvet or a good old hot water bottle. Such spinsters are most vulnerable in cold seasons. For most married men, their weakness is revealed when they are on trips away from home. In the confines of a cosy hotel, many miles away from home, their lusts become lord.

What is instructive is that you should do the right thing at the right time with the right people and in the right place. Joseph found himself in the wrong place, with the wrong person, at the wrong time and almost did the wrong thing until he took to his heels. If you are mindful of the thing, the time, the place and the person you will be free.

PRINCIPLE III: SENSITIVITY

The third number in the combination lock is an unmet need. You must of necessity know your unmet needs. Some vulnerable women may have lost out on having a father or a fatherly figure around them when they were little. Now that they are grown up, they are defenceless before any man that cares.

A lady once confessed that she was always attracted to older men with gray hair until Jesus destroyed that yoke in her life. For some other ladies, it could be to older men with dark hair. Yet another set of ladies could be obsessed with men who wear certain colours, colognes and the like. Our predilections vary. You must know yours so as to know when not to start what you cannot finish.

Most men, who did not have maternal figures around to affirm or support them when they were younger, become adult males susceptible to the charms of older women. If you can understand your combination you will know how to measure your vulnerability and how best to avoid the enemy's entrapments.

The clarion call is that for you to overcome the surge of sexual traps that permeate our world today you must be sensitive inside out. Mentally balanced people just do not wake up with the deliberate intent to commit life-threatening errors, but those who do are often people who do not see the beginning from the end and vice versa. Being a Christian is not enough; you must exercise every covenant caution in your daily walk with God and with men. There is an enemy out there whose main assignment from the foundation of the world is to steal, kill and destroy. Will you allow the evil one to frustrate your stay here on this earth and yet render you unworthy for the Kingdom of God?

There is a God-implanted conscience in you that essentially acts as a guide, a friend and a counsellor. If and only if you will obey your inner instinct, you will not only avert the errors of today, but also prepare the ground for a peaceful tomorrow. As it is often said, prevention is better than cure.

Prayer Points against the Assignment of Defilement

Defilement - Pray against the roots of the spirits of adultery, fornication, homosexuality, lesbianism, pornography and incest.

Prayer

Father Lord I receive power to be cleansed of defilement. I break every soulish and sexual tie (1 Corinthians 6:16) with anyone that is not my spouse today in Jesus name. I sever myself from every inordinate affection – Colossians 3:5; and I receive power going forward to resist the lure of temptations and to stand firm in the face of temptation like Joseph. Help me to be sensitive to and discern the plans of the enemy and to flee from sin - James 4:6-8. Create a clean heart in me - Psalm 51:10, Let my thoughts and the meditations of my heart be pleasing to you. Do not let sin have dominion over me in Jesus name - Romans 6:14. Amen.

Scriptures for Prayer

Psalm 51:10
Create in me a clean heart, O God and renew a steadfast spirit within me.

Psalm 19:13
Keep back Your servant also from presumptuous sins; Let them not have dominion over me. Then I shall be blameless and I shall be innocent of great transgression.

Romans 6:14

For sin shall not have dominion over you, for you are not under law but under grace.

1 Corinthians 6:16

Or do you not know that he who is joined to a harlot is one body with her? For "the two," He says, "shall become one flesh."

1 Corinthians 6:18

Flee sexual immorality. Every sin that a man does is outside the body, but he who commits sexual immorality sins against his own body.

Philippians 4:7-9

Finally, brethren, whatever things are true, whatever things are noble, whatever things are just, whatever things are pure, whatever things are lovely, whatever things are of good report, if there is any virtue and if there is anything **pr**aiseworthy—meditate on these things.

Colossians 3:5

Mortify therefore your members which are upon the earth; fornication, uncleanness, inordinate affection, evil concupiscence and covetousness, which is idolatry.

James 4:6-8

Therefore submit to God. Resist the devil and he will flee from you.

Do you not know that the unrighteous will not inherit the kingdom of God? Do not be deceived. Neither fornicators, nor idolaters, nor adulterers, nor homosexuals, nor sodomites, 10 nor thieves, nor covetous, nor drunkards, nor revilers, nor extortioners will inherit the kingdom of God. 11 And such were some of you. But you were washed, but you were sanctified, but you were justified in the name of the Lord Jesus and by the Spirit of our God. (1 Corinthians 6:9-11)

3It is God's will that you should be sanctified: that you should avoid sexual immorality; 4that each of you should learn to control his own body[a] in a way that is holy and honourable, 5not in passionate lust like the heathen, who do not know God; (1 Thessalonians 4: 3-5)

CHAPTER FIVE

DIVORCE
(MARITAL STRIFE)

The Facts

According to Drs. Tim Clinton and John Trent in their book *"Marriage and Family Counselling"* 2% of marriages last up to their 5th anniversary, 65% remain together until their 10th anniversary, 52% make it to their 15th, 33% to their 25th anniversary and 20% to their 35th and only 5% make it to their 50th anniversary.

- 80% of Pastors say they have insufficient time with their spouses[27]
- 80% of Pastors believe the Pastoral ministry affects their families negatively.[28]
- 24% of Pastors have received Marital Counselling.[29]
- 13% of Pastors have been divorced.[30]

SATAN ATTACKS FAMILIES

One area that the enemy has focussed a lot of his efforts on in order to do maximum damage is the area of marriage. His primary objective is to destroy the family structure and integrity. The family is the basic unit or foundational building block of every society. If you destroy the family, you destroy the refuge, support and springboard that undergird the child. The family is supposed to be a place of nurture, protection, development and inspiration. It is the breeding ground for the next generation of citizens and leaders of every society. It is commonly said that if we fail to build better homes, we will have to build bigger prisons.

SATAN ATTACKS MINISTERS AND THE CHURCH

The Church is the enemy's second most important target because it is "the pillar and the ground of truth"- 1 Timothy 3:15. The Church is also a beacon of hope to the hopeless, a place of healing and refuge to the hurting and family to the broken, rejected and disenfranchised. People from broken, unstable and abusive homes can find healing, comfort and a new identity, direction and family in the church. This is why the church has become the focus of the enemy's attack. The enemy invests a lot of his energies into attacking high profile Ministers and their marriages. He knows if he can focus his resources on breaking the Pastors' marriages it will have a domino and ripple effect on the parishioners and onlookers' marriages and eventually their families. Unfortunately, in the last

---

[38] London, H.B. Jr., (2003) Pastors at Greater Risk, Gospel Light Publications

[39] London, H.B. Jr., (2003) Pastors at Greater Risk, Gospel Light Publications

[40] London, H.B. Jr., (2003) Pastors at Greater Risk, Gospel Light Publications

[41] London, H.B. Jr., (2003) Pastors at Greater Risk, Gospel Light Publications

five years, I have personally seen close to 10 high profile international Ministers go through divorce.

WHAT ARE THE MAJOR CAUSES OF DIVORCE?

The increase in income is supported by greater activation of societal movements. These in turn impact the laws of the land. In today's date, laws of the westernised States have made it easier for an individual seeking divorce to fulfil his or her wishes in the given context. Yet, there are several underlying reasons for the steep increase in the rate of divorce.

James Walsh, a freelance writer, in an article[31] on how to get a quickie-divorce, gives several reasons for divorce. The following is culled in part and adapted from the article.

1. Infidelity

Infidelity, or an extra marital affair, is a major cause of the increase in divorce (it accounts for 17% in the US). The new age society has got numerous different avenues which enable people to get closely acquainted. There is increased interaction in the workplace. The regular fitness clubs and gymnasiums also provide chances of greater interaction with others.

In this day and age of mobile telephony and Internet chatting, it is much easier and simpler to make friends and remain in constant touch with them. All these combined may result in lesser time for one to spend with his or her spouse and greater interaction with outsiders. This is one of the major causes for an increase in extramarital affairs and its consequent impact upon the rate of divorce.

2. Communication Breakdown

Keeping your resentments simmering within, is another marriage destroyer, with the result that your partner does not come to know what is happening with you and this is likely to create distance between you and your partner.

3. Incompatible Personalities, Cultures, Interests and Aspirations

This is said to account for about 47% of divorces in the U.S. Couples who were once so in love and inseparable (can) grow totally apart because of the pressured lifestyles and disparate working life patterns.

4. Financial Problems

In today's fast paced life, money plays an important role, perhaps more today than ever before in history. As men mingle, the status of an individual is increasingly determined by material wealth. A lack of the ability to keep abreast with their peer group in this regard may cause unnecessary and avoidable stress on the married life of any two people. Even otherwise if there is a dearth of money to meet the basic household expenses, there is bound to be a lot of friction between the husband and wife on this account. Any intolerable increase in finance related troubles could also lead to divorce.

5. Work, Time and People Pressure

The modern day lifestyle is full of pressures on all fronts. There may be pressures at the workplace, peer pressures to have a better lifestyle and so on. This may result in an individual living at a very stressful pace.

As the stress accumulates, people automatically search for avenues to let out the steam. The easiest avenue is one's spouse. Thus a small issue may turn into a big fight and it may result in a breakdown in communication and lack of intimacy for many days, weeks, or months. This could lead to the erosion of the joy and peace in a marriage and could eventually lead to the destruction of the marriage itself.

6. Physical Abuse and Emotional Abuse

Long term physical abuse can be a major factor in the decision to file for divorce. As discussed in the last point, this can often result from a stressful lifestyle as well as poor conflict resolution skills.

Emotional abuse is distinct from its physical version. Nevertheless it can have far reaching consequences for the sufferer. The scars of emotional abuse may not be visible but they can be so deep so as to mar one's personality for a lifetime. There can be several causes of emotional abuse. It may be rooted in jealousy, a personality dysfunction or issues stemming from low self esteem. Irrespective of the causes behind it, emotional abuse can be a truly traumatic experience. This is another major factor in the breakup of marriages.

7. Mental Illness and Disease

The National Health Service reports that one in four people in the UK has a mental health problem at some point in their life which can affect their daily life, relationships or physical health. A woman who is suffering with depression will find it hard to be totally presentable to her husband and to build her marriage in a positive way. Likewise, a man suffering from schizophrenia is not healthy enough to be a loving husband in a consistent way. While some mental health issues are a result of chemical imbalance and can easily be addressed by prescription drugs, some have a spiritual root. The enemy will often step in where there is dejection or fear and inject hopelessness or severe anxiety which can mess up an individual's life and marriage.

8. Abandonment, Food, Alcohol, Sexual Addiction, Substance Abuse

Addiction is a relationship destroyer because it takes over the life of the addict and can make it very hard to live with them. Many addicts live only to feed their addiction and spend much of their time planning how to feed their addiction, As a result, key relationships are often neglected. Often, addicts will also act in other ways that destroy relationships such as stealing, lying to or cheating on those they love in order to feed their addiction. Addiction is a key tool of the enemy for the destruction of this generation.

9. Different expectations about household roles and responsibilities

When expectations do not match regarding who should be doing what in the marriage it affects the relationships. Dissatisfaction sets in because expectations are not met and conflicts ensue because spouses refuse to adjust or sacrifice their expectations.

10. The Inability to Manage or Resolve Conflict

Many people are unable to manage and resolve conflict and handle personality differences or what they may call 'irreconcilable differences'; either due to immaturity or because they do not have the skills to do so.

11. Religious Beliefs, Cultural and Lifestyle differences

Married couples with different religions, traditions and cultural values usually clash unless they are highly adaptive or accommodating. When couples are unable to work around these differences, it can lead to divorce after some time in the marriage.

12. Poor Communication

Lack of communication or poor communication is one of the leading causes of divorce. A marriage is on the rocks when the lines of communication fail. An individual cannot have an effective relationship with someone else if either he or she will not discuss feelings and cannot talk about mutual or personal issues. Keeping resentments simmering and under wraps; expecting one's partner to guess what the problem is, is a recipe for disaster.

13. Age at Time of Marriage and Family Background

People who come from divorced homes are more likely to get divorced than people who come from households in which their parents stayed together.[32] Divorce seems less of a big deal if you have seen your parents go through it and the enemy has an opening to start a negative generational pattern.

Research also shows that people who get married between the ages of 23-27 are more likely to stay together than people who get married in their teens[33]. Interestingly, people who cohabit before marriage have higher rates of divorce than people who did not cohabit before marriage.[34]

14. Pressures and Storms in Marriage

Storms do not create the problems in marriages; they come to reveal the cracks and problems already in the marriages' foundations.
Every marriage will face the occasional "thunder storm" which come but eventually blow away. Over the lifetime of a marriage, some marriages will face dangerous storms on the grade level of

---

[43] Common causes and reasons for divorce (article)

[44] Common causes and reasons for divorce (article)

[45] Common causes and reasons for divorce (article)

Hurricane Katrina as they confront issues like infidelity, prolonged infertility, financial insolvency and chronic infirmities (sickness). Very few marriages are able to remain standing for long after the wake of such storms. The enemy takes advantage of these storms to cause individuals to blame each other, sow resentment and unforgiveness.

These incidents need not break the marriage if we build according to God's pattern. (Read more about this in my book "*The Little Things that Make a Big Difference in Your Marriage*")

Signs and Symptoms of Impending Divorce

Marriage is no doubt something most people cherish, but there are times when partners cannot tolerate each other anymore. In such instances, divorce is often the next step.

- Constant complaints and comparisons with others.
- Irritability is another factor. Partners tend to get irritated with each other's presence.
- Sleeping in separate bedrooms.
- Being over-critical of each other's mannerisms and tastes.
- Seeking the advice of others on how to make a success of their relationship.
- Constant conflict.
- Lack of quality time together:
- Growing apart in interests and aspiration.
- Infidelity.

If several of these points are present in your marriage, the enemy has a foothold in your marriage. You need to deal with it seriously with a combination of prayer and behavioural change. I encourage you to read Christian books on marriage and to seek counselling from an experienced Christian counsellor.

PRAYER POINTS AGAINST THE ASSIGNMENT OF DIVORCE

Divorce – Pray against any issues of impending divorce or prolonged marital issues, separation, or prolonged strife in marriage.

PRAYER

Father, I thank You that marriage is Your idea and is blessed by You. Right now I commit my marriage to You. I ask You to be the third person, holding my marriage together. I thank You that what You have joined together no man or woman will put asunder (Matthew 19:6). Right now I eject every intruder and person interfering with my marriage. I ask that You re-unite us and make us one (Matthew 19:6). Cause us to always be enraptured with each other's love (Proverbs 5:19). I ask O God, that You build our house (Psalm 127:1). I ask O God, that You make me a teachable and submitted wife or a loving leader as a husband. Let the fruit of the spirit be evident in my life – make me gentle, peaceful, kind, self controlled and faithful in Jesus name (Galatians 5:22). Amen.

Scriptures for Prayer

Matthew 19:6
So then, they are no longer two but one flesh. Therefore what God has joined together, let not man separate."

Malachi 2:16
For the LORD God of Israel says that He hates divorce, for it covers one's garment with violence," says the LORD of hosts. "Therefore take heed to your spirit that you do not deal treacherously with the wife of your youth."

Galatians 5:22
22 But the fruit of the Spirit is love, joy, peace, longsuffering, kindness, goodness, faithfulness, 23 gentleness, self-control.

Psalm 127:1
The **LORD builds** the **house**, they labour in vain who build it; unless the **LORD** guards the city, the watchman stays awake in vain.

Proverbs 5:19
As a loving deer and a graceful doe, Let her breasts satisfy you at all times; and always be **enraptured** with her love.

Chapter Six

Dysfunction (Rebellion)

The Facts

- 39% of jailed inmates lived in homes without fathers.[35]
- 70% of all juvenile in State Reformed Institutions come from fatherless home.[36]
- 53% of Pastors' wives say they have difficulties in raising children.[37]
- 35% of Pastors report that their children's walk with God is the biggest concern about their families.[38]

Lack of good parenting

This chapter addresses the issue of dysfunctional children and adults; that is children who become disobedient, rebellious and manifest antisocial behaviour and the lives of the parents who raise them.

Parenting is a very difficult task for which the majority of us are not trained or prepared. Even as a full-time job it is not for the fainthearted. Many of us have to do it alongside earning a living, maintaining a marriage and living. More often than not because of the many vicissitudes life throws at us, one or two of the balls may drop and something then suffers and eventually malfunctions. Sometimes, it's the children that fall through the crack and malfunction. When children are not raised well, Satan can gain entrance into their lives and they can become attention seekers, promiscuous, bullies, addicts, irresponsible, rude, violent, hateful and rebellious.

Causes of Dysfunction in Children

Broken children come from broken homes. Dysfunction could be caused by a myriad of issues from children raised in one-parent homes to parents who are careless or clueless (or both), as well as high placed, pressured and time-starved parents.

Dysfunction in the home can also be due to divorce (and the instability and emotional fallout that creates for a child), defilement (sexual abuse) or some sin or curse in the family which opens the door to a spirit of rebellion and disobedience. This in turn causes the child to become relationally cold, distant, disobedient and rebellious to authority figures including God and His laws (at the very least creates an unbelieving or distant heart towards God).

---

[46] Stringer, Doug, (1995) The Fatherless generation: Hope for a Generation in Search of Identity, Destiny Image
[47] Stringer, Doug, (1995) The Fatherless generation: Hope for a Generation in Search of Identity, Destiny Image
[48] London, H.B. Jr., (2003) Pastors at Greater Risk, Gospel Light Publications
[49] London, H.B. Jr., (2003) Pastors at Greater Risk, Gospel Light Publications

Dysfunctional parenting clearly has a negative effect on society as a whole. Have you ever wondered what kind of home people like Saddam Hussein, Hitler, Charles Manson and other serial killers, rapists, paedophiles, drug dealers and other rebellious people came from? A group of Yale behavioural scientists found crime-rates to be highest among children/adults who had been raised solely by women.[39] The authority and balance that a man often brings to the home was missing in these households. This confirms the adage that states, "If we fail to build <u>better </u>families, we will have to build <u>bigger</u> prisons." Dysfunctional children grow up to become dysfunctional adults.

DOOR TO A SPIRIT OF REBELLION

"So the LORD said to Cain, "Why are you angry? And why has your countenance fallen?

7 "If you do well, will you not be accepted? And if you do not do well, <u>sin lies at the door.</u> And its desire is for you, but you should rule over it."

8 Now Cain talked with Abel his brother; and it came to pass, when they were in the field, that Cain rose up against Abel his brother and killed him." (Genesis 4:6-8)

The above scenario is a good example of how a parent's sin creates a dysfunctional family setting which opens the door to a spirit of rebellion which could even result in murder and or other forms of anti-social behaviour.

TYPES OF DYSFUNCTIONAL PARENTS

NEGLIGENT PARENTS BREED DYSFUNCTIONAL CHILDREN

This example is illustrated in the story of Eli and his sons. A man of God who was negligent in the raising of his children with the result that they became very wicked men. We see the same thing play out in the life of the world renowned healing evangelist of the early 20th century, John G. Lake whose wife died of physical exhaustion from overworking. It is said that Lake's marriage suffered greatly because of his constant absence. Apparently, even when present in the room, he would drift away in meditation, as he was constantly thinking of the Ministry and the Lord. As a result of this, his children felt greatly neglected and developed very hard and hardened attitudes towards God and their father. I have used these examples to show that being a Christian doesn't automatically make you a good parent.

"Now the sons of Eli were corrupt; they did not know the LORD.
13 And the priests' custom with the people was that when any man offered a sacrifice, the priest's servant would come with a three-pronged flesh hook in his hand while the meat was boiling.
14 Then he would thrust it into the pan, or kettle, or caldron, or pot; and the priest would take for himself all that the flesh hook brought up. So they did in Shiloh to all the Israelites who came there.

---

[50] http://sweetcardomom.wordpress.com/tag/absent-fathers/

15 Also, before they burned the fat, the priest's servant would come and say to the man who sacrificed, "Give meat for roasting to the priest, for he will not take boiled meat from you, but raw."

16 And if the man said to him, "They should really burn the fat first; then you may take as much as your heart desires," he would then answer him, "No, but you must give it now; and if not, I will take it by force."

17 Therefore <u>the sin of the young men was very great before the LORD,</u> for men abhorred the offering of the LORD."(1 Samuel 2:12-17)

"In that day I will perform against Eli all that I have spoken concerning his house, from beginning to end.

13 "For I have told him that <u>I will judge his house forever</u> for <u>the iniquity which he knows,</u> because <u>his sons made themselves vile and</u> he did not restrain them.

14 "And therefore I have sworn to the house of Eli that the iniquity of Eli's house shall not be atoned for by sacrifice or offering forever." (1 Samuel 3:12-14)

The above scriptures are evident of the kind of rebellious and disobedient heart that comes with dysfunction and how the Lord abhors it. Today these kinds of acts are termed 'anti-social behaviour'.

ABUSIVE PARENTS

On the news, we regularly hear of children who grow up in abusive homes. The abuse could be anything from verbal to physical or sexual abuse. Many children usually come out badly damaged from these experiences and are scarred for life. They will usually live with a constant sense of suspicion, distrust and disrespect for authority figures. The world is viewed as a dangerous and unstable place to live in by these children. Those whom God gave them to as gifts to care for and to nurture, have become instruments the enemy used as a source of evil, betrayal, pain and exploitation. Children who have been abused often become abusers or end up marrying abusers such that it becomes a vicious cycle and instigates a familial and generational pattern of abuse.

ADULTEROUS PARENTS

Adultery has serious damaging effects not only on a marriage but also on the children and the peace in a family. Infidelity will often cause arguments and the atmosphere of strife and tension at home creates a climate of insecurity for the children and could begin to affect their behaviour and sometimes their academics. These children may grow up rebellious because the kids feel the parents have been a bad example and not worthy of their respect. Sometimes children also live with a sense of embarrassment because of the adultery. Even worse can be the lot of the child born of an adulterous affair. Such a child can be subject to social stigma and wrestle with feelings of being a mistake or unwanted all their lives. These childhood traumas are fertile ground for the enemy to sow deep anger, hatred and rebellion.

ABSENT PARENTS

Parents become absent from a child's life as a result of death, divorce, work, emotional distance or just plain neglect. Regardless of the cause the effect is usually the same.

Some researches have indicated that the absence of good fathering is a contributor to the homosexual condition.[40] Don Schmierer in his book, "*An Ounce of Prevention*", further states that parents can also damage their children if they are present at home but are emotionally absent e.g. wrapped up in their own world, addicted to drugs, always on the phone or computer or simply emotionally inept or unreachable by their children. Dr. Arnold Nicholi's[41] research found that an emotionally or physically absent father contributes to a child's low motivation for achievement, inability to delay gratification, low self-esteem and susceptibility to group influence. This could lead to juvenile delinquency.

AUTOCRATIC PARENTS

These are the parents who are very controlling and overbearing. They are usually very demanding of their children and make almost every life decision for their children. They rule with an iron-hand. They may not be physically, verbally or sexually abusive but they are definitely mentally oppressive. This usually breeds feelings of resentment and lack of control in a child which may eventually lead to rebellion in the child in an effort to express and be their true self.

ADDICTED PARENTS

The effect of a parent's addiction to drugs, alcohol, smoking, gambling or sex is not just a bad example to the child but also shows the child that the parents are not consistent with their teachings and that they live a "Do what I say not what I do" life. The effect of addicted parents on children is diverse and far reaching; but in many

[51] Schmierer, Don, (2005) An Ounce of Prevention: Preventing the Homosexual Condition in Today's Youth, Promise Pub Co

[52] Nicholi, Armand M. Dr., Changes in the American Family. Family Research Council, nd.

it creates a sense of insecurity and vulnerability for the child. Children raised by addictive parents can often end up in addictions themselves – once again giving Satan the opportunity to operate generationally in a family.

ANAEMIC (WEAK) PARENTS

These are parents who are too weak to establish boundaries and enforce discipline and correction. They let the children off lightly on every offense so that they grow up spoilt and without having a sense of right and wrong. Eli and his sons discussed earlier best exemplify this.

ABDICATING PARENTS

I recently watched an episode of the Oprah Winfrey show in which she interviewed Todd Bridges on how he went from being an international child TV comedy show star to a drug addict and dealer. He was sexually abused at the age of 11 years by another man, but he was more scarred and traumatised by the wound from his father who called him a liar when he told him about the incident of sexual molestation. He felt abandoned and disappointed at his father for not standing up to defend him in his vulnerability. This experience opened up a valve of need for love and significance which he filled with drugs.

WHAT KIND OF PARENT ARE YOU?

Parents must take the task of parenting seriously- the consequences of not doing so are great. God has tasked us with caring for and raising children in the fear of the Lord. It is important to give some thought to what kind of parents we are and to ask how we can improve so that we can raise children who will become confident, secure, happy and responsible adults. Being a parent requires more than feeding, clothing and putting a roof over their head and sending them off to school. As a parent I must be concerned about my child's:

- Devotional life and walk with God
- Educational development
- Physical wellbeing
- Emotional wellbeing
- Friendships and associations
- Pastimes and interests
- Influences and exposure
- Aspiration and goals

Get knowledge in these areas – spend time with your children and get to know their needs, read books on parenting and attend seminars to become a better parent. May God help us all in this task!

PRAYER POINTS AGAINST THE ASSIGNMENT OF DYSFUNCTION

Pray against any issues of dysfunction e.g. disobedience, rebellion, insubordination, bad family background, anti-social behaviour and bullying.

Prayer

Father Lord, I come to You for help in this great task of raising children. Father I ask that You make my home a happy and a positive one for my children. Help me to build a home for them that is secure and stable in Jesus name. Father please teach me how to direct them in Your ways and teach them to fear You (Deuteronomy 6:7). Help me to raise them to be respectful and responsible. Help me to stir up the gift that is on the inside of each child and to help him or her achieve their destiny in You (2 Timothy 1:6).

Father I pray for the healing of any incident that has already wounded them. Father I ask that You would be a balm to them and cause them to forgive those transgressions. Do not let their personalities or life be marred in anyway. Bring Pastors, counsellors, teachers, friends and people into their lives that will build them up and reinforce them – not destroy them. I declare that the enemy will not kill them on the birthing stool and that they will overcome every plan of the enemy for their lives. I say every agenda of the enemy for their lives will fail in Jesus name. Sin will not have dominion over them in Jesus name (Genesis 4: 6-7). My children are for signs and wonders in their generation (Isaiah 8:18). I declare that it is well with them in Jesus name. Amen.

(If you have survived abuse of any kind in childhood, you can also pray this prayer for yourself).

Scriptures for Prayer

6 So the LORD said to Cain, "Why are you angry? And why has your countenance fallen? 7 If you do well, will you not be accepted?

And if you do not do well, sin lies at the door. And its desire is for you, but you should rule over it." (Genesis 4: 6-7)

Psalms 68:6

God places the **lonely** in families; he sets the prisoners free and gives them joy. But He makes the rebellious live in a sun-scorched land.

Psalm 68:5-7

A father of the fatherless, a defender of widows, Is God in His holy habitation.

God sets the solitary in families; He brings out those who are bound into prosperity; but the rebellious dwell in a dry land.

Joel 2:28

[*God's Spirit Poured Out*] " And it shall come to pass afterward That I will pour out My Spirit on all flesh; **Your** sons and **your** daughters shall prophesy, **Your** old **men** shall dream dreams, **Your young men** shall see visions.

But He answered and said, "Every plant which my heavenly Father has not planted will be uprooted. (Matthew 15:13)

Proverbs 29:17

Correct your son and he will give you rest; yes, he will give delight to your soul

2 Timothy 1:6

Therefore I remind you to stir up the gift of God which is in you through the laying on of my hands.

Deuteronomy 6:7

You shall teach them diligently to your children and shall talk of them when you sit in your house, when you walk by the way, when you lie down and when you rise up.

Isaiah 8:18

Here am I and the **children** whom the LORD has given me! We are for **signs** and **wonders** in Israel from the LORD of hosts, who dwells in Mount Zion.

SECTION 3

MIND
BOMBARDIERS

CHAPTER SEVEN

DEJECTION
(REJECTION AND
LOW SELF-ESTEEM)

The Facts

- 70% of Pastors say they have a lower self-esteem now than when they started out in ministry. [42]

Rejection and low self-esteem are rampant in our society. So many people feel 'less than', inferior or invaluable. This is due to a poor self-image. Self-image has been described as: 'the <u>mental</u> picture (generally of a kind that is quite resistant to change) that depicts not only details that are potentially available to objective investigation by others (<u>height</u>, <u>weight</u>, <u>hair colour</u>, <u>gender</u>, <u>I.Q. score</u>, ...), but also items that have been learned by that person about himself or herself, either from personal experiences or by <u>internalizing</u> the judgments of others. A simple definition of a person's self-image is their answer to this question - "What do you believe people think about you?"'[43] So a poor self-image is one that is negative, poor or low.

ONE MAN'S STORY

The story of Mephibosheth in the Bible is a great illustration of someone with low self-esteem or poor self-image.

"Then the king said, "Is there not still someone of the house of Saul, to whom I may show the kindness of God?" And Ziba said to the king, "There is still a son of Jonathan <u>who is lame in his feet</u>."
4 So the king said to him, "Where is he?" And Ziba said to the king, "Indeed he is in the house of Machir the son of Ammiel, in Lo Debar."
5 Then King David sent and brought him out of the house of Machir the son of Ammiel, from Lo Debar.
6 Now when Mephibosheth the son of Jonathan, the son of Saul, had come to David, he fell on his face and prostrated himself. Then David said, "Mephibosheth?" And he answered, "Here is your servant!"
7 So David said to him, "Do not fear, for I will surely show you kindness for Jonathan your father's sake and will restore to you all the land of Saul your grandfather; and you shall eat bread at my table continually."
8 Then he bowed himself and said, "<u>What is your servant, that you should look upon such a dead dog as I?</u>"
9 And the king called to Ziba, Saul's servant and said to him, "I have given to your master's son all that belonged to Saul and to all his house.
10 "You therefore and your sons and your servants, shall work the land for him and you shall bring in the harvest, that your master's son may have food to eat. <u>But Mephibosheth your master's son shall</u>

eat bread at my table always." _Now Ziba had fifteen sons and twenty servants." (2 Samuel 9:1-10)_

In this story, we see how he had been born a prince into a palace but in the political wranglings involving his father he had been injured and became lame. He went from the palace to the pit and was raised in obscurity. When King David eventually offered Mephibosheth a place of honour at his table, he didn't feel worthy to receive it – he saw himself as a dead dog. Its one thing to refer to oneself as a dog, but a dead one really takes the biscuit! This response shows how low his self-image was.

CAUSES OF LOW SELF-ESTEEM/POOR IMAGE

There are various causes and reasons for low self-esteem. It can be due to:
- Accumulated criticisms collected over the years which have led to damaging view of oneself. Children in particular are vulnerable to accepting negative judgments from authority figures because they are yet to develop the ability to sort out the wheat from the chaff.
- Observing others around us and deducing that we don't match up to them for some reason or the other and are thus inferior in some way or other. For example a person may struggle with low self-esteem due to status – feeling one is of a 'lower class' or hasn't achieved as much as one's peers.
- Traumatic experiences such as rape, molestation, physical or mental abuse.

---

[55] http://en.wikipedia.org/wiki/Self-esteem_instability

- Extreme deprivation – growing in an atmosphere without access to many amenities or opportunities can create a feeling of being 'less than' those who grew up with all the things they needed.

Further causes were highlighted in a study by Kamakura[44] . He states 'Factors including over-reliance on the evaluations, love and approval of others; an impoverished self-concept and excessive dependency needs produce feelings of little self-worth resulting in highly unstable individuals. Furthermore, developmentally harsh or controlling family environments were thought to promote fragile, unstable feelings of self-worth. Possessing a well-developed self-concept is also implicated in optimal psychological functioning. When self-knowledge is confused and conflicted it will fail to provide meaningful input into people's behaviours and reactions …'

WOMEN AND LOW SELF-ESTEEM

Women you are not what you weigh!!! The media has told women they only look beautiful and sexually attractive if they are thin but are ugly and undesirable if you are not.

BEAUTY AT TOO HIGH A PRICE

Magazines say you are 'it' if you have the latest designer bag and clothes. When some women look in the mirror there is an image they desire to see (like the one in the magazines). When they don't see that image - they can feel inferior in some way and are enticed to buy the 'right' clothes, accessories and so on to get 'the look' and feel ok. Sometimes, it's the car they drive or the neighbourhood they live in or having the right accent that they think will make them valuable. Of course, this is a recipe for disaster and a door to another type of bondage - debt.

DO YOU THINK I AM BEAUTIFUL?

Cybil Shepherd, a very famous model and actress hated the emphasis on just her looks, body and sexuality with little or no acknowledgement of her worth as a person. She felt diminished in her self-worth even though she was a top model who appeared regularly on the covers of Glamour and Vogue magazine.

In truth most of us are not limited in life by whom or what we think we are but rather by who or what we think we are not.

SOME SYMPTOMS AND SIGNS OF LOW SELF-ESTEEM

1. Inability to see yourself 'squarely' - to be fair to yourself.
2. A never ending feeling of not being good enough.
3. Inability to accept genuine compliments from people.
4. An insatiable appetite for the affirmation of others.
5. Always seeking the affirmation of others and external validation.
6. Exaggerated concern over what you imagine other people think.
7. A hypersensitivity to the passing remarks of others.
8. A desire to always buy new things to help you gain acceptance from others.
9. An inordinate desire for position and recognition and other status symbols.
10. Flirting with people of the opposite sex to feel desirable and important.

11. Reluctance to trust your own opinion.

12. Accentuating only the negative aspects of your life.

13. Anxiety and emotional turmoil.

14. Lack of social skills and self confidence.

15. Fear of revealing our real self to others.

16. An unhealthy comparison and competition with others.

According to Lisa Bevere[45], most of us have a projected and protected image.

DAMAGING EFFECTS OF LOW SELF-ESTEEM

DIFFICULT RELATIONSHIPS

A poor self-image in one or both lovers can have very damaging effects on the love and the trust bond in the relationship. People with low self-esteem find it extremely difficult to receive love because they feel unworthy and unlovable and as a result find it difficult to give love themselves. They can easily feel insecure in the relationship - thinking of or assuming negative things that are not true which makes them feel threatened in the relationship. As a result, confusion and strife will be commonplace in that relationship.

WOMEN AND THEIR RELATIONSHIPS

According to Shelly Adams[46], a woman's low self-esteem can affect every relationship she has. She may feel unworthy as a daughter, feeling she let her parents down by not being as successful, smart, or popular as a sibling, or to the same degree that she feels her parents think she should be. As a wife, she may not feel pretty enough, thin enough, or sexually attractive enough. She may even marry someone who is mentally or physically abusive, as she feels she doesn't deserve more. As a parent herself, she may have difficulty being a strict disciplinarian. In friendships, she may not pursue any relationships, causing her to feel more isolated. She may be a pushover and be unable to say no. She may develop relationships with people who take advantage of her vulnerability.

DOMESTIC ABUSE

Self-esteem issues also arise in studies of domestic abuse. Husbands who abuse their wives usually come from less affluent backgrounds, had poorer education or earned less money than their wives; violence is used as a way to assert their 'superiority' and put their "uppity" wives in their place. Another study found that men who earned high academic qualifications but had poor careers were exceptionally violent as a group; perhaps because they were frustrated their lives did not reflect their high opinions of themselves. By contrast, men who had poor education but nonetheless had very successful careers were six times less likely than average to be abusive[47].

---

[56] Bevere, Lisa (1998). You are not what you weigh: Escaping the lie and living the truth. Lake Mary, FL: Creation House.

[57] Adams, Shelley, Signs of Low Self-Esteem in Women

[58] Baumeister, R. F., (1997). Evil: Inside human violence and cruelty. New York: W.H. Freeman., 1997)

Eating Disorders

Eating disorders such as anorexia nervosa and bulimia nervosa are rife among young women. Anorexia Nervosa is characterised by refusal to maintain a healthy body weight and an obsessive fear of gaining weight. Bulimia Nervosa is characterised by recurrent binge eating followed by compensatory behaviours such as purging (self-induced vomiting or excessive use of laxatives). The causes of eating disorders are complex and poorly understood, but research[48] does indicate that peer pressure and idealised body-types seen in the media are a significant factor in causing eating disorders. Girls literally starve to death because of a desire to be someone other than they are because they don't like who they are.

An Endangered Generation

Results of a study by Kamakura[49] indicated that environmental factors played a significant part in stability in self-esteem. This buttresses what we have discussed this chapter - that the home environment, childhood experiences and nature of relationship with parents are key determinants of self-esteem and value. Yet, so many families' lifestyles leave much to be desired.

- 77% of teenagers say their mothers are hardly ever home when they return from school.[50]
- Half of today's young people have lived through the divorce.[51]
- 50-60% of young people in the US grow up in single parent homes.[52]
- 70% of all juveniles in State reform institutions come from homes without a father.[53] (SWDYTYA).
- Girls raised in foster care are many times more likely to develop bulimia nervosa.[54]

Satan is very aware of the great potential that resides in our children and the importance of the home life in bringing it out. He is not oblivious to the treasure and gift that God has deposited in each child. He knows that if these children grow up in wholesome, loving environments they will become a major threat to his kingdom. Love and affection are as crucial to humans as water and sunlight are to plants such that their absence negatively affects the proper development and functioning of the human personality. One of Satan's most effective strategies is to deprive people of the love, security and nurturing environment required for their proper mental, physical and emotional development. His arsenal is always aimed at damaging and destroying children. His strategy is to deprive them of the love, security and nurturing environment required for their proper development. He launches his attacks on individuals at all stages of life, as they journey from the womb to the tomb.

How can we counteract this devilish scheme that threatens the sanity of the coming generation? Is there any provision in Scripture for the reversal of this downward trend?

[59] Hudson et al. The prevalence and correlates of eating disorders in the National Co morbidity Survey Replication.[Biological Psychiatry. 2007 Feb 1;61(3)348-58 PMID 16815322]

[60] http://en.wikipedia.org/wiki/Self-esteem_instability

[61] Willard Harley Jr., Women and Infidelity, (article)

[62] London, H.B. Jr., (2003) Pastors at Greater Risk, Gospel Light Publications

[63] Fola-Alade, Sola, Dr., (2003) So, Who Do You Really Think You Are? How to Heal the Wounds of the Past and Reveal the Real You. Vision Media

[64] Fola-Alade, Sola, Dr., (2003) So, Who Do You Really Think You Are? How to Heal the Wounds of the Past and Reveal the Real You. Vision Media

[65] http://en.wikipedia.org/wiki/Eating_disorder

Healing low self-esteem

The Remedy for low self-esteem is Unconditional love.

Mother Teresa is reported to have said, "The biggest disease in the world today is not leprosy or tuberculosis, but rather the feeling of being deserted (rejected), neither wanted nor cared for by anybody." At the heart of the human problem is the problem of the human heart. We desperately need love. When we are loved we feel valued, significant, important and special. Just as it is negative experiences and the absence of love that cause low self-esteem; it is love and affection that reverse it. "We must receive the warmth of human love and assurance if we are to blossom and expose the unique beauty and talent that God has placed within each and every one of us."[55]

Sometimes, God will start a process of healing low self-esteem by bringing someone into our life who will demonstrate true love and affection and help us to feel valued and special. A friend, a husband, a pastor can be used by God to shore up our esteem, build us up and begin a work of reparation in our life. Often, He steps in Himself, as we study His Word we discover our value in Him. We discover how much He loves us and the price He paid for us. When we know this love deeply in our heart, not just in our head, it transforms us.

Christian therapy can also be very helpful in dealing with low self-esteem. Through therapy one can be helped to understand the root of dejection/depression. A good therapist will also help a client suffering with low self-esteem to discover a sense of personal value and worth.

Also crucial can be the support of friends or a small group of believers where one is valued and cared for - to give a sense of acceptance and belonging which can be so crucial for healing low self-esteem.

PRAYER POINTS AGAINST THE ASSIGNMENT OF DEJECTION

Dejection - Pray against low self-esteem, poor self-image, inadequacies, insecurities and inferiority complex.

PRAYER

Father, I know I am not a mistake, because before I was formed You knew me - **Jeremiah 1:5**. I am Your special creation – created for good works which You purposed before the foundation of the world. I worship You because I am fearfully and wonderfully made- **Psalm 139:14**. I thank You because You love me with an unrelenting, fierce and passionate love. Thank You for showing me how important I am to You by dying for me - **John 3:16**. I thank You because I am valuable and precious to You and You will never leave me or forsake me - Hebrews 13:5.

---

[66] Fola-Alade, Sola, Dr., (2003) So, Who Do You Really Think You Are? How to Heal the Wounds of the Past and Reveal the Real You. Vision Media

SCRIPTURES FOR PRAYER

I can do all things through Christ who strengthens me.
(Philippians 4:13)

Psalm 139:14
"I will praise you, for I am **fearfully** and **wonderfully made**;
marvellous are your works and that my soul knows very well."

Jeremiah 1:5
"Before I formed you in the **womb** I knew you; ..."

Jeremiah 31:3
"The LORD has appeared of old to me, saying: 'Yes, I have loved
you with an **everlasting love**; Therefore with loving-kindness I
have drawn you."

John 3:16
"For God so loved the world that He gave His only begotten Son,
that whoever believes in Him should not perish but have everlasting
life."

Hebrews 13:5
He Himself has said, "I will never **leave** you nor **forsake** you."

Romans 8:37
'...in all these things we are more than conquerors through Him
who loved us. [38] For I am persuaded that neither death nor life, nor
angels nor principalities nor powers, nor things present nor things
to come, [39] nor height nor depth, nor any other created thing, shall
be able to separate us from the love of God which is in Christ Jesus
our Lord'.

CHAPTER EIGHT

DEPRESSION
(DISCOURAGEMENT)

The Facts
- 19 million adults are said to be suffering from depression.[56]
- People born after 1950 are ten times more likely to experience depression than their predecessors.[57]
- Women are twice as likely to experience depression as men.[58]
- 2 out of every 3 hospital beds in the US are occupied by people with mental problems.[59]
- Depression is the common cause of mental illness.
- Suicide is the highest killer of 18-21 year olds in the US.[60]
- Suicide is the fourth leading cause of death in youngsters between the ages of 10 and 14 years.[61]

WHAT IS DEPRESSION?

Depression is a condition of general emotional dejection and withdrawal; sadness greater and more prolonged than that warranted by any objective reason. A depressed person is also a discouraged person. Discouragement is a feeling of despair, sadness or lack of confidence. A discouraged person is disheartened. A depressed person often loses interest in things they used to enjoy. Depression commonly interferes with work, social and family life. The enemy can weigh in and magnify issues and problems such that a person feels overwhelmed and unavailable to go on in life.

There are two major types of depression[62] and three levels of depression.

Two major types of depression

1. Reactive Depression: This is caused by many life issues including stress, anger, rejection, guilt, failure, loneliness, loss, grief, family issues, or divorce. With this type of depression, the symptoms may be lowest in the morning and increases as the day progresses.

2. Endogenous Depression: These are generally caused by medical and biological factors such as an inherited predisposition, female hormonal fluctuations, serotonin irregularities, thyroid abnormalities, diabetes, Vitamin B12 or D

---

[67] http://www.promises.com/depression-anxiety.php
[68] www.ecounseling.com/online_counseling/15-depression
[69] http://www.womens-menopause-health.com/Depression/depress_statistics.htm
[70] http://www.namigc.org/content/fact_sheets/generalInfo/PublicAction/web-information-for-writers-on-mi-0304.htm
[71] http://www.benbest.com/lifeext/causes.html
[72] http://www.teensuicidestatistics.com/
[73] http://www.netdoctor.co.uk/diseases/depression/classification_000001.htm

or iron deficiency, lack of sunlight, prescription drug induced depression (Antihypertensive, Oral contraceptives) and recreational drug induced depression (Alcohol, Marijuana, Cocaine). With this type of depression, sufferers feel worse in the morning.

THREE LEVELS OF DEPRESSION

The UK National Health Service categorises and describes depression by how serious it is as follows:

- **Mild depression:** has some impact on your daily life.
- **Moderate depression:** has a significant impact on your daily life.
- **Severe depression:** makes the activities of daily life nearly impossible. A small proportion of people with severe depression may have psychotic symptoms.

GRIEF AND DEPRESSION

Even though grief and depression share many of the same characteristics, there are important differences between them. Grief is an entirely natural response to a loss, while depression is an illness. However, sometimes, it can be hard to distinguish between feelings of grief and depression.

People who are grieving find that feelings of loss and sadness come in waves, but they are still able to enjoy things and are able to look forward to the future. However, those who are depressed have a constant feeling of sadness; they do not enjoy anything and have little sense of a positive future.

DEPRESSION AND SUICIDE

Even when depression begins to abate, much attention is needed as there is some indication that depressed people are more at risk of suicide after depression starts to abate. Dr. Tim Clinton and Ron Hawkins[63] say suicide is the tragic and lethal end of a psychological process that results from unresolved events that create depression and hopelessness. A person who was inert with depression may become decisive with new energy - enough energy to commit suicide.

BIBLICAL EXAMPLES

There are a number of important examples in scripture, such as Naomi's story after she lost her husband and two sons in Moab and Elijah's saga with Jezebel.

> *"19 Now the two of them went until they came to Bethlehem. And it happened, when they had come to Bethlehem that all the city was excited because of them; and the women said, "Is this Naomi?"*
> *20 But she said to them, "Do not call me Naomi (Sweet); call me Mara (Bitter), for the Almighty has dealt very bitterly with me.*
> *21 "I went out full and the LORD has brought me home again empty. Why do you call me Naomi, since the LORD has testified against me and the Almighty has afflicted me?""(Ruth 2:19-21)*

This was one lady who had been through a lot. After a move to a new city, she lost her husband and two sons. This also meant she

---

[74] Clinton, Tim, Dr. & Hawkins, Ron, Dr., (2009) The Quick reference Guide to Biblical Counselling, Baker Books

lost her retirement plan (as in those days, the responsibility for her upkeep after her husband's death would have been that of her sons). Naomi found herself alone in a strange city with no resources and seemingly without a future. It is not surprising that she became bitter, hopeless and empty about her life and future.

"And Ahab told Jezebel all that Elijah had done also how he had executed all the prophets with the sword.
2 Then Jezebel sent a messenger to Elijah, saying, "So let the gods do to me and more also, if I do not make your life as the life of one of them by tomorrow about this time."
3 And when he saw that, <u>he arose and ran for his life and</u> went to Beersheba, which belongs to Judah and left his servant there.
4 But he himself went a day's journey into the wilderness and came and sat down under a broom tree. And <u>he prayed that he might die</u> and said, "It is enough! Now, LORD, take my life, for I am no better than my fathers!"
5 Then as he lay and slept under a broom tree, suddenly an angel touched him and said to him, "Arise and eat.""(1 Kings19:1-5)

After many battles fought alone Elijah was ready to throw in the towel – for good. Even warriors can feel defeated – when they war alone for too long. It can be lonely at the top and the pressures are enormous.

CAUSES AND RISK FACTORS FOR DEPRESSION

Experts believe that depression is caused by a combination of biological, psychological and social factors. In other words, one's lifestyle choices, relationships and coping skills matter just as much if not more so than genetics. However, certain risk factors can make one more vulnerable to depression.

- Loneliness
- Lack of social support
- Recent stressful life experiences
- Family history of depression
- Marital or relationship problems
- Financial strain
- Early childhood trauma or abuse
- Alcohol or drug abuse
- Unemployment or underemployment
- Health problems or chronic pain

The Most Stressful events in People's lives[64]

There appears to be a complex relationship among stressful situations, our mind and our body's reaction to stress and the onset of clinical depression. It is clear that some people develop depression after a stressful event in their lives. Events such as the death of a loved one, the loss of a job, or the end of a relationship are often negative and traumatic and cause great stress for many people. Stress can also occur as the result of a more positive event such as getting married, moving to a new city, or starting a new job. It is not uncommon for either positive or negative events to become a crisis that precedes the development of clinical depression.

The Holmes and Rahe Stress Scale (shown below) is a well-known tool for measuring the amount of stress you have experienced within the past year. Taking the test can help you see clearly if you are at risk of illness due to stress which can then lead onto depression.

	Life Event	Value	Check if this applies
1	Death of spouse	100	
2	Divorce	73	
3	Marital separation	65	
4	Jail term	63	
5	Death of close family member	63	
6	Personal injury or illness	53	
7	Marriage	50	
8	Fired at work	47	
9	Marital reconciliation	45	
10	Retirement	45	
11	Change in health of family member	44	
12	Pregnancy	40	
13	Sex difficulties	39	
14	Gain of new family member	39	
15	Business readjustment	39	
16	Change in financial state	38	
17	Death of close friend	37	
18	Change to a different line of work	36	
19	Change in number of arguments with spouse	35	
20	A large mortgage or loan	31	
21	Foreclosure of mortgage or loan	30	
22	Change in responsibilities at work	29	
23	Son or daughter leaving home	29	
24	Trouble with in-laws	29	
25	Outstanding personal achievement	28	
26	Spouse begins or stops work	26	
27	Begin or end school/college	26	
28	Change in living conditions	25	

29	Revision of personal habits	24
30	Trouble with boss	23
31	Change in work hours or conditions	20
32	Change in residence	20
33	Change in school/college	20
34	Change in recreation	19
35	Change in church activities	19
36	Change in social activities	18
37	A moderate loan or mortgage	17
38	Change in sleeping habits	16
39	Change in number of family get-togethers	15
40	Change in eating habits	15
41	Vacation	13
42	Christmas	12
43	Minor violations of the law	11

Your Total

Note: If you experienced the same event more than once, then to gain a more accurate total, add the score again for each extra occurrence of the event.

Score Interpretation

Score   Comment

300+   You have a high or very high risk of becoming ill in the near future.

150-299   You have a moderate to high chance of becoming ill in the near future.

<150   You have only a low to moderate chance of becoming ill in the near future.

Once you have taken the test, if you find that you are at a moderate or high level of risk, then an obvious first thing to do is to try to avoid future life crises. While this is clearly easier said than done, one can usually avoid moving house, for example, close to when retirement is due or when a child is about to go off to college. One can also learn **conflict resolution skills** to minimise conflict with other people; avoid taking on new obligations or engaging with new programmes of study. Last but not least, it's important to take things easy and look after oneself.

SYMPTOMS OF DEPRESSION[65]

HOW DO YOU KNOW IF YOU ARE DEPRESSED?

Psychological symptoms
- Continuous low mood or sadness,
- Feelings of hopelessness and helplessness,
- Low self-esteem,
- Fearfulness,
- Feelings of guilt,
- Feeling irritable and intolerant of others,
- Lack of motivation and little interest in things,
- Difficulty making decisions,
- Lack of enjoyment,
- Suicidal thoughts or thoughts of harming someone else,
- Feeling anxious or worried and
- Reduced sex drive.

Physical symptoms
- Slowed movement or speech,
- Change in appetite or weight (usually decreased, but sometimes

increased),
- Constipation,
- Unexplained aches and pains,
- Lack of energy or lack of interest in sex,
- Changes to the menstrual cycle and
- Disturbed sleep patterns (for example, problems going to sleep or waking in the early hours of the morning).

Social symptoms:
- Not performing well at work,
- Taking part in fewer social activities and avoiding contact with friends,
- Reduced hobbies and interests and
- Difficulties in home and family life.

If you have identified that you or someone you know is suffering with depression, it is important to take the right steps quickly.

REMEDIES FOR DEPRESSION

- Identify the root cause: biological, medical, psychological, social or spiritual causes and deal accordingly.
- Go for a full medical check up including checks for hormonal imbalance.
- Arrange to see Mental Health Practitioner or therapist.
- Ensure the proper social support from friends and or family.
- Encourage rest, relaxation and recreation.
- Encourage physical fitness.
- Seek spiritual counsel and prayers and possibly deliverance.

---

[76] http://www.nhs.uk/Conditions/Depression/Pages/Symptoms.aspx

PRAYER POINTS AGAINST THE ASSIGNMENT OF DEPRESSION

Depression - Pray against the spirit of shame, guilt, discouragement, accusations and insanity.

PRAYER

Father, I thank You because I have a future and a hope in You. I thank You because I know You have a good plan for my life - **Jeremiah 29:11**. Right now I break every spirit of despondency, darkness and heaviness lingering over my life - **Isaiah 61:3**. I break it in Jesus name. I cancel every satanic appointment to reinforce disappointment and depression in my life. Father, please send the right people to help me in Jesus name – the right therapists, helpers and friends. I claim Your Word and declare that I will go from victory to victory, from faith to faith and from grace to grace in You. I will not die but live to declare the goodness of the Lord in the land of the living. It is well with me in Jesus name. Amen.

SCRIPTURES FOR PRAYER

Isaiah 61:3
"To console those who mourn in Zion, to give them beauty for ashes, the oil of joy for mourning, the garment of praise for the spirit of heaviness; that they may be called trees of righteousness, the planting of the LORD, that He may be glorified."

Romans 15:13
"Now may the God of hope fill you with all joy and peace in

believing, that you may abound in hope by the power of the Holy Spirit."

Jeremiah 29:11
"For I know the thoughts that I think toward you, says the LORD, thoughts of peace and not of evil, to give you a **future** and a **hope**."

Job 11:17
"And your life would be brighter than noonday. Though you were dark, you would be like the morning."

Proverbs 4:18
"But the path of the just is like the shining sun, that shines ever brighter unto the perfect day."

CHAPTER NINE

DECEPTION

The Facts

- When placed in a situation where lying is in a child's self-interest (to avoid punishment), children as young as age two-and-a-half will lie to get out of trouble[66].
- All but two percent of teenagers in a recent US study admitted lying to their parents[67].
- Out of 36 possible topics – including drug use, dating and their friends – the average teen lied regarding 12 of them[68].
- During a bogus experiment on ESP (a mind-reading task), people are presented with an opportunity to cheat in order to win a $50 prize. When people are placed in such a situation, almost everyone cheats (90%) and then when confronted about their behaviour, few tell the truth; only 9% to 20% of the individuals in these studies confess when questioned[69].

WHAT IS DECEPTION?

Deception has been described as beguilement, bluffing, mystification and subterfuge to propagate beliefs that are not true, or not the whole truth (as in **half-truths** or omission). Deception can involve **propaganda** and **sleight of hand** can employ distraction, camouflage or concealment. There is also **self-deception**. Lying is as old as time and seems to be something we don't need to be taught to do; and probably everybody alive has lied at some point or the other.

Deception began in the Garden of Eden.

"Now <u>the serpent was more cunning</u> than any beast of the field which the LORD God had made. And he said to the woman, "Has God indeed said, 'You shall not eat of every tree of the garden'?"

2 And the woman said to the serpent, "We may eat the fruit of the trees of the garden;

3 "but of the fruit of the tree which is in the midst of the garden, God has said, 'You shall not eat it, nor shall you touch it, lest you die.'"

4 Then <u>the serpent said to the woman, "You will not surely die.</u>

5 "For God knows that in the day you eat of it your eyes will be opened and you will be like God, knowing good and evil."

6 So when the woman saw that the tree was good for food, that it was pleasant to the eyes and a tree desirable to make one wise, she took of its fruit and ate. <u>She also gave to her husband with her and</u>

---

[77](http://www.truthaboutdeception.com/lying-and-deception/how-often-lovers-lie/experiments.html

[78] http://www.preventionaction.org/research/liars-learned-lies-%E2%80%93-and-statistics

[79] http://www.preventionaction.org/research/liars-learned-lies-%E2%80%93-and-statistics

[80]http://www.truthaboutdeception.com/lying-and-deception/how-often-lovers-lie/experiments.html

he ate.

7 Then the eyes of both of them were opened and they knew that they were naked; and <u>they sewed fig leaves together and made themselves coverings.</u>

8 And they heard the sound of the LORD God walking in the garden in the cool of the day and <u>Adam and his wife hid themselves</u> from the presence of the LORD God among the trees of the garden."(Genesis 3:1-8)

Whilst we may lie, we don't like to be lied to. Deception is a major **relational transgression** that often leads to feelings of betrayal and distrust between people. Deception violates relational **rules** and is a **violation** of expectations. Most people expect friends, lovers and even strangers to be truthful most of the time. However, on any given day, it is likely that most human beings will either deceive or be deceived by another person. A significant amount of deception occurs between romantic and relational partners.

Young children most often lie to avoid punishment, but reasons for lying become more complex as they grow up. Lying is a way to increase power, manipulate peers, get attention and smooth social relationships. If a child is still lying a great deal at age seven and it has become a successful strategy for handling social situations, then he or she is likely to continue to lie a lot throughout childhood according to research[70].

THE PRIMARY FORMS OF DECEPTION

The five primary forms of deception are:[71]

1. **Lies:** making up information or giving information that is the

opposite or very different from the truth.

2. **Equivocations**: making an indirect, ambiguous, or contradictory statement.

3. **Concealments**: omitting information that is important or relevant to the given context, or engaging in behaviour that helps hide relevant information.

4. **Exaggeration**: overstatement or stretching the truth to a degree.

5. **Understatement:** minimisation or downplaying aspects of the truth.

The Reasons for Deception

In his book titled 'Love busters', Willard Harley Jr., highlights four types of dishonesty:

1. **Protector liars:** This happens when a person tries to protect another person from feeling hurt by withholding their true feelings or unpleasant information. The problem is that it really does not protect, but rather denies the "protected" crucial information. Examples of this are withholding information about a tragedy of financial loss, or true feelings about someone else.

2. **Trying to look good liars:** Some people are in such great need of admiration and approval that they try to make themselves look better than they really are by exaggerating their accomplishments and creating false impressions. Most of us like to put our best foot forward; an example of this is lying on job application forms.

3. **Avoid-trouble liars:** People who lie to avoid the consequence of having done something wrong. For example, lying to conceal an affair.

4. **Born (compulsive) liars:** These people basically lie about everything whether good or bad. They usually live double lives. It is usually difficult to reform this kind of person because they rarely see it as a problem. For example, con artists and fraudsters.

CAUSES OF DECEPTION

Whilst lying is commonplace, there is no denying its roots are evil. John 8:44 identifies lying as being of the devil. It states -

'You belong to your father, the devil and you want to carry out your father's desires. He was a murderer from the beginning, not holding to the truth, for there is no truth in him. When he lies, he speaks his native language, for he is a liar and the father of lies.'

When we lie we are giving in to Satan and opening the door to him to wreak havoc. Often, one lie has to be followed with another to cover up the previous lie and before an individual knows it, they are in deep trouble. Also, lies are often a result of sin; people lie to cover up wrong or bad actions. So the enemy tempts us into sin and when we yield, he'll also tempt us to lie to cover up. I am not saying the devil *makes* us lie, but he does tempt us and we can *decide* to yield; sometimes with disastrous results. Sometimes people have woven such an intricate web of lies that when it's discovered it causes irreparable damage to relationships and lives.

Lies that Lovers Tell each other

The following "list of lies" comes from a survey of dating and married couples who were asked to disclose the issues they try to keep hidden from their partners through lies, concealment and deception[72].

Relational Issues

- Time Together - people lie about the reasons why they cannot spend time together or see each other ("I am so busy, I have so much work to do, I don't have time right now").
- Past Relationships - partners lie about their past level of involvement ("I never really loved her," "I am much closer to you," "I love you so much more than anyone else").
- Feelings, Interest, Crushes and Attraction to Others - people lie about their feelings and interest in others - often includes ex-partners, friends, someone at work.
- Secret Contact - lovers lie about their friendships, time spent with others, accidental encounters (running into an ex), phone calls, e-mails and text messages with others. Essentially people lie about intimate, but non-sexual contact with someone else.
- Levels of Commitment – people lie about their feelings for partner, uncertainty or doubts about the relationship – e.g. they may not be sure they really love or want to marry a partner or stay together.
- Flirting with others - people lie about flirting with others.
- Betraying confidences - lovers lie to each other about keeping secrets confidential.

---

[72] This survey was conducted by and culled from www.oasis.com

- Hide time with others - people hide activities and time spent with others - usually friends or co-workers.

Negative Thoughts

- Negative Feelings towards Partner's Family/Friends – e.g. people lie about liking other people who are important to a partner.
- Negative Feelings about Partner's Physical Appearance - e.g. lovers lie about liking their partner's appearance, hair, weight, age or clothes.
- Negative Feelings about a Partner's Career - e.g. people lie about liking or respecting their partner's job, school or career choices.
- Negative Feelings about a Partner's Behaviour or Character - e.g. lovers lie about liking their partner's kids, habits, personality or sense of humour.
- Hide Others' Negative Feelings about Partner - people lie about other people's true feelings towards a partner (e.g. saying my family and friends like you when they don't).

Negative Behaviours

- Drug Use - lovers lie about past or current drug use.
- Alcohol Consumption - partners lie about alcohol consumption.
- Smoking - people lie about smoking.
- Gambling - lovers lie about gambling.

Differences

- Hide Important Beliefs - lovers lie about their true feelings on issues such as politics, religion or pets in order to get along with partner.
- Enjoyment of Activities - people lie about enjoying things a partner likes to do.

Financial Issues

- Resources - people lie about their income, resources, inheritance.
- Debt - lovers lie about their level of debt.
- Spending Habits - people lie about how they spend money.

Insecurities

- Physical Appearance/health - people lie about their age, weight, health.
- Jealousy - lovers lie about being jealous and snooping.
- Career Performance - partners lie about how well their work, school or career is going.
- Family and Friends - lovers lie to make family and friends seem better.
- Love and Emotions - people lie to their partners about feeling vulnerable, scared and being overly emotional.

The Effects of Deception on a Marriage

Should you really tell your Partner everything about yourself?

Willard Harley Jr., says, It is this sort of confusion that leads some of the most well-intentioned husbands and wives to lie to each other, or at least give each other false impressions. They feel that dishonesty will help them protect each other's feelings. But what kind of a relationship is that? The lie is a wall that comes between the two partners; its something hidden, a secret that cannot be mentioned, yet it is right under the surface of every conversation. Dishonesty can be as addictive as a drug. One secret leads to another. If you start using dishonesty to protect each other's feelings, where will it end? Lies clearly hurt a relationship over the long-term, but truth can also hurt, especially in the short-term. It is no wonder that many couples continue in dishonesty - because they feel they cannot take the shock of facing the truth, at least right now. As a result, the marriage dies a slow death. Honesty is like flu shot. It may give you a short, sharp pain, but it keeps you healthier over the following months.

Infidelity is an extreme example of something people would be tempted to lie about. But "little white lies" can be just as destructive when discovered and there is even less justification for them. If it makes sense to be honest about something as hurtful as an affair and it makes even more sense to be honest about something more trivial, such as buying something you know your spouse would not have approved of.

Dishonesty may defer some of that pain, but it compounds the pain later. The truth usually comes out eventually and the months or years of hiding it not only creates an emotional barrier before it is revealed, but also destroys trust afterward.

THE REMEDY TO DECEPTION IS RADICAL HONESTY

Willard Harley Jr., continues that, honesty is the only way that a husband and wife can ever truly come to understand each other. Without honesty, the adjustments that are crucial to the creation of compatibility in a marriage cannot be made. Without honesty, the best efforts to resolve conflicts will be wasted because each spouse will not understand each other well enough to find mutually acceptable solutions.

Granted, dishonesty can be a good short-term solution to marital conflict. It will probably get one off the hook for a few days or months or keep the problem on the back burner. But it is a terrible long-term solution. If you expect to live with your spouse for a while and still be in love, dishonesty can get you into a great deal of trouble.

What is Radical Honesty?

Revealing to your spouse as much information about yourself as you know, including your thoughts, feelings, habits, *likes, dislikes*, personal history, daily *activities and* plans for the future.

To help explain this policy, Harley Jr., further breaks Radical Honesty down into

1. **Emotional Honesty:** Revealing your emotional reactions, both positive and negative, to the events of your life, particularly to your spouse's behaviour.

2. **Historical Honesty:** Revealing information about your personal history, particularly events that demonstrate personal weakness or failure.

3. **Current Honesty:** Revealing information about the events of your day and providing one's spouse with a calendar of one's activities, with special emphasis on those that may affect your spouse.

4. **Future Honesty:** Revealing your thoughts and plans regarding future activities and objectives.

The Effects of Deception on Society

Not only does deception destroy homes and break up marriages; deception costs society in fraudulent activity and criminal behaviour that's covered up. Of course the recent financial crisis of a worldwide collapse of the banking system is an example of the results of deception on a grand scale. It is reported that the FBI has opened investigations into more than 500 cases of alleged corporate fraud, including 38 that involve major firms and are "directly related" to the national <u>economic crisis</u>[73]. FBI Deputy Director John Pistole told Congress.

Demonic Deception

Not only does Satan cause people to deceive others, he also causes people to be deceived. As I write this I am watching a documentary about a former rabbi who is 'married' to seven women. He believes God told him to marry them. As I watched bewildered I listened to the real pain of the seven women who were struggling with jealousy and low self-esteem because of the situation. They all looked tired and haggard. One of them explained that she had wanted to leave but felt that if she wanted to receive from God she had to sacrifice by enduring the relationship. How sad and what a marred picture of God. This sort of deception must delight the enemy – that is always his agenda- to distort God's picture and instructions to His people (that's what he did with Eve).

Another young man has written a book about the 'down low' phenomenon (a trend among some African-American men to have sex occasionally with other men whilst in a marriage or committed relationship with a woman). In this book he details his frequent sexual encounters with both men and women whilst claiming to be a Christian and committed church member. His rationale is that since God gave him free will and knew what he would do even before he does it; God can then subsequently not judge him for exercising the free will that He gave him. This details the extent of man's deception. Needless to say his lifestyle is a risky one, rife with sexually transmitted disease's (and sometimes death due to HIV/Aids), divorce and confusion for any children married to men on the down low. And of course the one who came to kill, steal and destroy is delighted.

The thief does not come except to **steal** and to **kill** and to **destroy**. I have come that they may have life and that they may have it more abundantly. John 10:10

The key to deliverance from this kind of deception is the word of God – the bible. When we study the bible we discover real truth and God's desire for His creation. His plan for marriage is one man and one woman – simple. Multiple wives and sexual partners of whatever sex are not His plan for mankind. The full and abundant life He has for us does not include STD's, Aids death, divorce and confused kids.

---

[84] Fraud 'Directly Related' to Financial Crisis Probed By JASON RYAN, ABC News Report, Feb. 11, 2009

Prayer Points against the Assignment of Deception

Deception – Pray against false and other religions, new age, Islam evolution and racism.

Prayer points

Father, today I ask that You help me to be truthful in all my dealings and interactions. Please help me to break every habit and tendency to lie. Help me to be mindful of my responses and to always tell the truth in Jesus name.

Right now I break every spirit of deception over my life. Father I ask that You would pierce their darkness with Your truth. Break the power and sway of the enemy over their mind, thought, beliefs and life in Jesus name. I speak deliverance and declare that they will know the truth and that the truth will set them free.

Scriptures for prayer

1 John 2: 26-27
"These things I have written to you concerning those who try to deceive you. 27 But the anointing which you have received from Him abides in you and you do not need that anyone teach you; but as the same anointing teaches you concerning all things and is true and is not a lie and just as it has taught you, you will abide in Him".

Micah 7:8
"Do not rejoice over me, my enemy; when I fall, I will arise; when

I sit in **darkness**, The LORD will be a **light** to me."

Matthew 6:23
The people who sat in **darkness** have seen a great **light** and upon those who sat in the region and shadow of death, Light has dawned."

John 8:12
Then Jesus spoke to them again, saying, "I am the light of the world. He who follows Me shall not walk in darkness, but have the light of life."

Acts 26:18
"To open their eyes, in order to turn them from darkness to light and from the power of Satan to God, that they may receive forgiveness of sins and an inheritance among those who are sanctified by faith in Me."

Hebrews 10:22
"Let us draw near with a true heart in full assurance of faith, having our hearts sprinkled from an evil conscience and our bodies washed with pure water."

Philippians 4:8
Finally, brethren, whatever things are true, whatever things are noble, whatever things are just, whatever things are pure, whatever things are lovely, whatever things are of good report, if there is any virtue and if there is anything praiseworthy— meditate on these things.

SECTION 4

SPIRITUAL POISONS

CHAPTER TEN

DESTRUCTION

The Facts

- 2 women are killed each week by a current or former partner.[74]
- 1 woman in 9 is severely beaten by her male partner each year.[75]
- 1 in 4 women will be a victim of domestic violence in their lifetime – many of these on a number of occasions.[76]
- In 90% of domestic violence incidents, children were in the same or the next room.[77]
- In over 50% of known domestic violence cases, children were also directly abused.[78]
- Murder is the leading cause of death for <u>African-American</u> males aged 15 to 34.
- In 2006, FBI's Supplementary Homicide Report indicated that most of the 14,990 murder victims were Black.
- An estimated 520,000 people were murdered in 2000 around the globe. Two-fifths of them were young people between the ages of 10 and 29 who were killed by other young people.

Anger is one of Satan's key Weapons of Mass Destruction

We can hardly turn on the news today without learning of another murder, rape or terrorist incident. These are violent times and the key emotion behind these vile activities is anger. Anger can make a good person do very destructive things. There is a self-destructive and devastating effect for others of harbouring anger and planning revenge. The scripture below shows how uncontrolled anger can become destructive.

"6 So the LORD said to Cain, "Why are you angry? And why has your countenance fallen?
7 "If you do well, will you not be accepted? And if you do not do well, sin lies at the door. And its desire is for you, but you should rule over it."
8 Now Cain talked with Abel his brother; and it came to pass, when they were in the field, that Cain rose up against Abel his brother and killed him." (Genesis 4:6-8)

What is Anger?

Anger is a God-given powerful emotion with an intensity that ranges from frustration to severe fury. It can last for as long as a few seconds to a life-time. Anger by itself is not sin, it is our response thereafter that determines whether it becomes sin or not.

---

[85] http://refuge.org.uk/get-help-now/what-is-domestic-violence/domestic-violence-the-facts/
[86] http://refuge.org.uk/get-help-now/what-is-domestic-violence/domestic-violence-the-facts/
[87] http://www.womensaid.org.uk/domestic_violence_topic.asp?
section=0001000100220036&itemTitle=Statistics
[88] http://refuge.org.uk/get-help-now/what-is-domestic-violence/domestic-violence-the-facts/
[89] http://refuge.org.uk/get-help-now/what-is-domestic-violence/domestic-violence-the-facts/

CAUSES OF ANGER

Anger by itself, is not the real problem, but an indicator like a red warning light on a car dashboard that there is something wrong with a part of the engine.

In the same way, according to Dr. Tim Clinton[79], anger is usually a response to a person, a situation, or event (imaginary or anticipated) or to memories of traumatic or enraging situations. He elaborates that it could also be a response to a real or perceived injustice or hurt in the form of frustration, betrayal, deprivation, injustice, exploitation, manipulation, criticism, disapproval, jealousy, humiliation or intimidations.

According the Chip Ingram in his book "Overcoming Emotions that Destroy", the causes of anger can be grouped into three general categories.

Unmet expectations: Anger manifests itself as a feeling of frustration when a certain goal or aspiration or expectation we have set eludes us; when our plans are thwarted and an appointment is missed or hopes are dashed. *A Biblical example is Moses anger when he came down from the mountain and discovered that the Israelites had backslidden into idol worship.*

So it was, as soon as he came near the camp, that he saw the calf and the dancing. So Moses' anger became hot and he cast the tablets out of his hands and broke them at the foot of the mountain. (Exodus 32:19)

- **Unmet needs:** Anger may indicate that we have unmet needs and are feeling hurt. Generally as humans we have the need to be loved, accepted, affirmed, recognised and supported. When these needs are not met we feel hurt. This hurt could be expressed outwardly in the form of hostility, defiance or inwardly in the form of inner hurts disappointments, loneliness, rejection and feelings of betrayal.

- **Threatened sense of self:** Anger may also be a way of covering up our insecurity. Whether the threat is real or perceived and there seems to be an attack on your self-esteem we may feel humiliated, embarrassed and terrified. A Biblical example is King Saul's jealousy and insecurity when he discovered that David had developed quite a following for his military exploits.

"So the women sang as they danced and said: "Saul has slain his thousands and David his ten thousands."
8 Then Saul was very angry and the saying displeased him; and he said, "They have ascribed to David ten thousands and to me they have ascribed only thousands. Now what more can he have but the kingdom?"
9 So Saul eyed David from that day forward." (1 Samuel 18:7-9)

DIFFERENT EXPRESSIONS OF ANGER

Anger can be expressed in a number of ways and to different degrees.

1. Internalisation
Repression: This happens when people are angry but deny its presence. The anger is there even though it is undetected. This can

---

[90] Clinton, Tim, Dr. & Hawkins, Ron, Dr., (2009) The Quick reference Guide to Biblical Counselling, Baker Books

be quite dangerous and destructive to the person internalising it because the anger is turned inwards instead of outwards. This causes an implosion instead of an explosion. This is what causes many physical and emotional disorders like anxiety, depression, ulcers and high blood pressure.

Suppression: In this case, people recognise the anger but control it and channel its force into advancing other causes; while this can be potentially good it still ignores the cause and does not deal with the real root of the problem. The risk of suppression is that the anger tends to leak out, manifest or express itself in other forms e.g. cynicism, sarcasm, betrayal, maligning, rebellion and other forms of passive aggressive attitudes.

2. Ventilation

Expression: Anger can either be expressed positively by addressing the real issues in a constructive manner through dialogue and non-aggressive methods of stating one's hurts and position and seeking resolve without a confrontation. The negative way of expressing one's anger is by verbal and or physical outbursts, violence and revenge. These forces then become externally destructive to others and society at large.

LEVELS OF ANGER

IRRITATION

The act of troubling or annoying someone or provoking them. A Biblical example is the rivalry between Hannah and Peninah.
"And her rival also <u>provoked her severely</u>, to make her miserable, because the LORD had closed her womb." (1 Samuel 1:6)

Indignation

This occurs when one is angered at something wrong or unjust and feels that the wrong must be corrected. It is sometimes called "Righteous Anger". An example of this in the Bible is Nehemiah's anger that the well-off in Israel were taking advantage of the less well-off by charging exorbitant interest.

"And I became very angry when I heard their outcry and these words.7 After serious thought, I rebuked the nobles and rulers and said to them, "Each of you is exacting usury from his brother." So I called a great assembly against them." (Nehemiah 5:6)

Resentment

Is a feeling of deep and bitter anger or ill-will towards another person.

Wrath

Is a strong desire for revenge. Absalom secretly hid a strong desire for revenge for Amnon's rape of his sister until the right time.

"And Absalom spoke to his brother Amnon neither good nor bad. For Absalom hated Amnon, because he had forced his sister Tamar."(2Samuel 13:22)

Fury

A partial loss of emotional control and a state of mental agitation. David was furious on hearing the story of a man whose choice pet lamb was commandeered from him by a powerful man, until he found out that he was the powerful man and the lamb was Uriah's wife, Bathsheba that he had slept with.

"5 So David's anger was greatly aroused against the man and he said to Nathan, "As the LORD lives, the man who has done this shall surely die!" (2 Samuel12:5)

RAGE

A loss of control involving aggression or an act of violence.

HOSTILITY

A persistent form of anger or enmity toward others that becomes rooted in one's personality, which affects one's entire outlook on the world and life. Some people have been angry for so long that anger is not an occasional thing like it is for most people - they are perpetually angry. They have been aggrieved so deeply and for so long that anger now marks them and much of their responses.

EFFECTS OF ANGER ON THE ANGRY

Anger by itself is not bad if controlled and positively harnessed. However, if it is harboured and allowed to fester over a long time it could cause harm to the individual both physically and emotionally.

PHYSICAL SYMPTOMS

Quite a number of medical conditions have been attributed to persistent anger, such as headaches, ulcers, hypertension, colitis, arthritis, heart diseases and cancer.

EMOTIONAL SYMPTOMS

The emotional by-product of persistent anger is a critical attitude, being sarcastic, impatient, unforgiving and wicked.

EFFECTS OF ANGER ON FAMILIES

An unresolved state of anger among members of a family can easily progress into verbal abuse, physical abuse, domestic violence, divorce, rebellion, or even murder. Unchecked and unresolved anger is a time bomb waiting to explode. Take the story of the Mendes brothers. One night, the boys' fury exploded and they shot their mother and father several times in their family sitting room, alleging years of sexual abuse by them. Unresolved anger is dangerous.

EFFECTS OF ANGER ON SOCIETY

People are angry and their anger is increasingly costly and destructive to society. From road rage to violent assaults outside pubs to teenage knife crime – the consequences of anger for society are easily evident.

To show you the various types of hate crimes that could come from the root of anger I have taken liberty to quote the definition from California's DUI Murder Law in order for you to get the picture of the effects of chronic unresolved anger on our society.

"Murder in the First and Second Degree (14-17) - A murder which shall be perpetrated by ... poison, lying in wait, imprisonment, starving, torture, or by any other kind of wilful, deliberate and premeditated killing or which shall be committed in the perpetration or attempted perpetration of any arson, rape or sex offense, robbery, kidnapping, burglary, or other felony committed or attempted with the use of a deadly weapon, shall be ... murder in the first degree ... and shall be punished by death or life imprisonment ... except that any person ... under 17 years of age at the time of the murder shall be punished with imprisonment ... for life. All other kinds of murder, including that which shall be proximately caused by the unlawful distribution of opium or any synthetic or natural salt, compound, derivative, or the preparation of opium ... cause the death of the user, shall be ... murder in the second degree and ... shall be punished as a Class C felony."

Satan loves anger because it gives him the opportunity to tempt people to destroy themselves and others.

OVERPOWERING THE DESTRUCTIVE SIDE OF ANGER

The key thing is to *identify the reason for anger and deal with it.* *Ephesians* **says** "Be angry and do **not** sin": do **not let** the **sun** go **down** on your wrath. The last part of that scripture is the key to victory over anger and to express and resolve anger quickly so that it doesn't build up and result in chaos.

The Biblical mandate is to approach those who upset us or who we have upset and look to resolve things amicably. If that fails we are to take others with us to help us in the attempt to make peace and as a last resort we are encouraged to get church leadership involved. The key principle here is that we are to make every effort to resolve upset and not leave matters lingering or stewing. It is when things are left unresolved that is dangerous because it gives the anger time to increase and for plots to be hatched.

Therefore if you bring your gift to the altar and there remember that your brother has something against you, [24] *leave your gift there before the altar and go your way. First be reconciled to your brother and then come and offer your gift. Matthew 5:23*

Another key part to managing anger is learning to forgive people. When we are unforgiving to people who have hurt us, it keeps us chained in a prison of bitterness and hatred. We must do all in our efforts to release those who have wronged us, no matter how grievous their behaviour. Even if you have to extend forgiveness several times until it becomes genuine in your heart – do so. It will save you poisoned relationships and ulcers later on and free you from being a tool of the enemy.

Prayer Points against the assignment of Destruction

Destruction: Pray against the roots of destruction which is anger, offence, bitterness, unforgiveness, jealousy, envy and their consequent effects such as violence and murder.

Prayer

Father, please help me to identify and resolve the root of anger in my life. I ask You to help me to forgive those who have offended me even as You forgive me for my transgressions. I break every stronghold of anger in my life and I bind every violent or destructive spirit that would attempt to work through me. I declare I will be able to manage my temper. I ask that You give me a gentle spirit which is not easily angered or provoked. I receive a spirit of self-control and ask that You help me to manage my reactions well. Spirit of the living God, release Your fruit in me – Galatians 5:22. I declare I am an agent for good and not for evil in Jesus Name.

Scriptures for Prayer

Ephesians 4:26
"Be angry but sin not…"

Matthew 5:44
"Pray for those who despitefully use you…"

Romans 12:21
"Overcome evil with good…"

Job 5: 21-22
"You shall be hidden from the scourge of the tongue and you shall not be afraid of destruction when it comes. 22 You shall laugh at destruction and famine and you shall not be afraid of the beasts of the earth."

Psalm 91: 6; 10
6 Nor of the pestilence that walks in darkness, Nor of the destruction that lays waste at noonday. 10 No evil shall befall you, nor shall any plague come near your dwelling.

CHAPTER ELEVEN

DRUGS (ADDICTION)

The Facts
- Teenage drinking in UK is almost the worst in Europe.
- Approximately 40% of all crimes are committed under the influence of alcohol.[80]
- In 2005 a total of 33,541 persons died of drug induced causes in the US.[81]
- 60% of men that attended Promise Keepers Men's conference said they struggled with pornography.[82]
- An average of 3 million adults meets the criteria for pathological gambling in the US.[83]

WHAT IS AN ADDICTION?

An addiction is a dependence on a substance (e.g. alcohol, prescription medicine, street drugs) or activity (e.g. gambling, shopping). The American Society of Addiction Medicine defines addiction as 'a primary, chronic disease of brain reward, motivation, memory and related circuitry. Dysfunction in these circuits leads to characteristic biological, psychological, social and spiritual manifestations. This is reflected in the individual pursuing reward and/or relief by substance use and other behaviours'.

Addiction is characterised by impairment in behavioural control, craving, inability to consistently abstain and diminished recognition of significant problems with one's behaviours and interpersonal relationships. It usually leads to activity that is designed solely to obtain the substance or activity to cover up its use e.g. the housewife addicted to shopping hiding the credit card statements and items bought, a drug-addict shoplifting to support the habit or a gambler embezzling to pay off debts.

Like other chronic diseases, addiction involves cycles of relapse and remission. Without treatment or engagement in recovery activities, addiction is progressive and can result in disability or premature death.

It is usually characterised by the defence mechanism of denial, where the addict blames his or her problem on someone else.

Addiction is characterised by:
Intense Cravings
- **Appetite**: A desire to satisfy any bodily need: an appetite for food or sex.
- **Craving**: A longing for, an eager desire, great longing e.g. to crave sweets or affection.
- **Lusts:** Uncontrolled or illicit desire or appetite; lecherousness.
Passionate or overmastering desire or craving: e.g. an insatiable lust

---

91 http://alcoholism.about.com/cs/costs/a/aa980415.htm
92 http://www.cdc.gov/nchs/data/nvsr/nvsr56/nvsr56_10.pdf
93 http://www.blazinggrace.org/cms/bg/pornstats
94 http://www.problemgambling.com/faq.html

for money.

An addiction is not an appetite, because our appetite is our body's natural way of informing us that we need something. Instead addiction starts with a strong craving for something and progresses into a lust for that thing that is so strong that it does not mind destroying itself or other people in the process of satisfying it.

The Israelites experienced cravings so strong that they were prepared to return to a lifestyle of bondage and oppression to satisfy their lusts.

"Now the mixed multitude who were among them yielded to intense craving; so the children of Israel also wept again and said: "Who will give us meat to eat?

5 "We remember the fish which we ate freely in Egypt, the cucumbers, the melons, the leeks, the onions and the garlic;

6 "but now our whole being is dried up; there is nothing at all except this manna before our eyes!"" (Numbers 11:4-6)

Types of Addictions

Addictions are as varied as there are people, there's one for everyone.

Drugs

Drug addiction is a pathological or abnormal condition which arises due to frequent drug use. The disorder of addiction involves progressively increased consumption of drugs and accompanying drug-seeking behaviour. As the addiction grows, the addict loses interest in many other things and drug use becomes his or her sole focus.

ALCOHOL

Alcoholism is a disabling addictive disorder. It is characterised by compulsive and uncontrolled consumption of alcohol despite its negative effects on the drinker's health, relationships and social standing. Like other drug addictions, alcoholism is medically defined as a treatable disease.

NICOTINE

Nicotine, a legal drug, is highly addictive (many studies have shown it to be more addictive than cocaine and heroin). It is so addictive because nicotine increases dopamine which is one of the key neurotransmitters actively involved in the brain. In effect, nicotine activates reward pathways—the circuitry within the brain that regulates feelings of pleasure and euphoria. Nicotine is hard to give up because of the pleasure it gives.

CAFFEINE

Caffeine, another commonly available and popular substance in the Western world is hugely addictive. In large amounts and especially over extended periods of time, caffeine can lead to a condition known as *caffeinism.* Caffeinism usually combines caffeine dependency with a wide range of unpleasant physical and mental conditions. Research has shown that drinking more than 500mg a day can cause the brain to become overactive, impairing concentration and performance. The effect on the brain can also make people feel jittery and agitated, moody and emotional. As caffeine has a direct effect on the heart, heart rate and blood pressure can soar, triggering palpitations, hyperventilating and sweating[84].

Food

Compulsive overeating, also sometimes called food addiction, is characterised by an obsessive or compulsive relationship to food. An individual suffering from compulsive overeating disorder engages in frequent episodes of uncontrolled eating, or binge eating, during which they may feel frenzied or out of control, often consuming food past the point of being comfortably full. Bingeing in this way is generally followed by feelings of guilt and depression.

Shopping

Compulsive buying disorder (CBD) is characterised by an obsession with shopping and buying behaviour that has negative consequences. Compulsive buying is not limited to people who spend beyond their means, it also includes people who spend an inordinate amount of time shopping or who chronically think about buying things but never purchase them. Most persons with CBD meet the criteria for an axis II disorder. CBD is found in 5.8% of the United States population.

Gambling

Problem gambling ("ludomania") is an urge to gamble despite harmful negative consequences or a desire to stop. Problem gambling often is defined by whether harm is experienced by the gambler or others, rather than by the gambler's behaviour. Severe problem gambling may be diagnosed as clinical.

Sex

Sexual addiction refers to the phenomenon in which individuals report being unable to manage their sexual behaviour. It has also been called sexual dependency and sexual compulsivity. The

[95] As reported by in The Sun newspaper, Women's health section, 16 August 2007

existence of the condition is not universally accepted by sexologists and its roots, nature and validity are still being debated.

LOVE

Love addiction is a human behaviour in which people become addicted to the feeling of love. Love addicts can take on multiple behaviours, but a common thread that runs through all love addicts is the love for the feeling of being in love. They crave the 'newness' and excitement that characterises the start of a relationship and the romantic feelings that's associated it. It is normal for the other person to be idolised by the love addict as at this stage of the relationship as they do not know them well enough to know their flaws and weaknesses.

The love addict then projects other kinds of illusions onto the other person and creates the picture of an ideal lover that is based on pure fantasy. The love addict will usually lose interest once the romantic stage of a relationship subsides as he or she begins to realise the 'ordinariness' of the other person. The love addict is unable or unwilling to deal with a real relationship and the work that it entails; they prefer the high of romantic love only.

PORNOGRAPHY

Pornography addiction can be defined as a dependence upon pornography, characterised by obsessive viewing, reading and thinking about pornography and sexual themes to the detriment of other areas of one's own life.

COMMON CHARACTERISTICS OF ADDICTIONS

Avoidance of Feelings: The addiction is usually used to improve the addict's emotional and psychological state. It is a way of avoiding feelings of loneliness, anxiety, anger or sorrow. It is also used to numb feelings of emotional pain.

Increasing Tolerance: There is an increased tolerance to the natural effects of the body's response to its own neurotransmitters and therefore the threshold for what produces pleasure is increased.

Progressive effect: Many begin by experimenting, but because more is needed of the same substance or activity to cause the same desired pleasurable, comfort or relief effect, the addict will increase addictive actions in strength and frequency.

Lack of Control: To the addict their dependency to the addiction is beyond their control.

Withdrawal Symptoms: A physiological withdrawal state is experienced when the substance is removed or abused.

Estrangement from God: The question is which came first the addiction or the estrangement? Habitual sin will keep us farther away from God. Distance from God increases the stronghold of the sin.

HOW DOES ADDICTION START?

According to Dr. John Marsden of BBC Health, people try drugs or other potentially addictive behaviour because they are seeking some sort of reward or benefit. Those who take drugs, for instance, do so because of the physical effects they hope to experience. Drugs have a marked effect on the body and mind. If there were no effect, people would be unlikely to repeat the experience. No one sets out to become addicted. Crucially, substances and certain behaviours change the way we feel. If they make us feel better, relax us, make us feel powerful, excite us, let us escape and so on, we tend to go back to them.

Sometimes, the attraction also comes from the feeling that the behaviour identifies us as one of a certain social group. People may try drugs because they think it will gain them acceptance in a desirable gang or that they become one of the rebels or cool party people.

However, in some people, those experiences uncover a powerful attraction. What can start out as casual experimentation, normal social behaviour or even a doctor's prescription can lead to repeating the behaviour more frequently and with greater quantities. The more you do, the more likely you are to do more.

SHIFT TO DEPENDENCE

Following the psychological shift to dependence (can't do without), the brain's chemistry may start to adapt, demanding even more of what it has grown used to and fiercely resisting the discomfort of withdrawal. The behaviour takes on a self-perpetuating life of its own as the body becomes physically dependent on it.

WHAT CAUSES ADDICTION?

What makes some people more susceptible to becoming dependent or addicted is perhaps a genetic predisposition. This theory, with some evidence to support it, makes sense especially since addiction crosses social divides. However, this is still debatable.

There are also cultural and social factors that put people at greater risk. For instance, you are less likely to become alcohol dependent growing up in a country where alcohol consumption is unacceptable than where it is a normal part of everyday life. Growing up in a family where there is alcohol or drug abuse increases the risk. This is also the case for people who suffer childhood trauma, abuse and neglect.

Poverty, a lack of education and unemployment can also increase the risks. If your environment is stressful and you feel unable to change it, you may turn to substances for relief. Significant life events may contribute. If your inner world is in turmoil, you may turn to substances as medication to feel better.

People who do not receive adequate nurture as children or who are more emotionally sensitive may be more susceptible. These factors will not always lead to substance misuse or dependency or any other addictive behaviour, but they can increase vulnerability.

Trauma, Emotional pain and deprivation

Addicts tend to come from families that have caused emotional, physical, sexual or spiritual wounds. They usually have feelings of deep sadness, shame and loneliness or a feeling of being deprived of love, affection or affirmation.

Many addicts feel lonely and abandoned, they really long for genuine love, affirmation and touch. The substance or behaviour then becomes a substitute for true love. Addicts also tend to suffer from intimacy disorder. They feel if their addictions were known by people, they would be hated and then deserted.

Dr. Tim Clinton in his book "Biblical Counselling" stated the following,

Relational: Addictive behaviour is positively related to troublesome early life relationships.

Emotional: Addicts are emotionally wounded. One study of Sex addicts found 81% to be sexually abused, 74% physically abused and 97% emotionally abused ("Don't call it love" by Mark and Debra Laser).

WHAT ARE THE RISK FACTORS?

Relational: For adults, addiction also causes stress in interpersonal relationships. It impairs relationships, reliability and responsibility.

Behavioural: Addicts behaviour is often challenging due to cravings and needs that the addiction creates. It can cause them to behave irrationally mentally and physically; and sometimes to pose harm to themselves and others.

Physical: Experience of pain (sometimes extreme) when they do not have access to the drug; also illness and death can result e.g. from drug, nicotine or alcohol addiction.

Spiritual: Addiction is essentially a rebellion against God. There may be an underlying disappointment, anger and lack of trust and faith in God. The addiction then becomes a false idol to the addict.

An addiction is yet another way that a person can open their life for the devil to run roughshod through it leaving disaster in his wake. Addicts have been known to lie, steal and even kill to get their substance of choice. Addicts have betrayed close friendships, left babies in dust bins and sold their bodies in prostitution. When addiction is severe addicts will go on a binge for days without any care for their personal wellbeing, safety or security or that of those who are close to them. From gamblers to drug, sex or love addicts, addicts' lives are ravaged and abused and the devil's plan is to strip it of as much value and meaning as possible.

How to treat Addictions

Many treatments for addiction are rarely ever totally successful, because they try to treat the symptoms without identifying the root cause.

Don't scratch that itch!

Seeking to treat addiction without addressing the root is like wanting to stop an itch without tackling the cause. In reality, the itch may be due to a rash which in turn might be the result of an allergic reaction. Until the cause of itch is identified and addressed, it will be pointless to expect the itch to stop. The bottom line is, if you treat the allergy, the rash will disappear and the need to scratch the itch will be no more. But as long as the allergy is untreated and the rash remains, scratching is the only way to achieve relief.

LOOKING FOR LOVE IN THE WRONG PLACES

This can be illustrated by the example of a lady abandoned by her father who never had anyone around in her life to nurture her and affirm her worth and esteem in her childhood. As a result, she may develop an intense craving for a man's love in her growing years as a result of the emotional deprivation she experienced in childhood. This intense craving for a man's attention and affirmation may be assuaged whenever she is in a relationship with a man (as she finds comfort and relief in it); but when she is not in a relationship she feels down, depressed and despondent.

As a result, such a woman could easily become relationship dependent, needing to be in a relationship to feel valuable. She could become addicted to the love and affection she gets from men which could lead to a craving so intense that causes her to want to get it at any cost, even if she has to give her body sexually in return for affection from any man in return for the temporary relief from the touch and affection shown her. This is essentially how a love addiction may develop into a sex addiction.

This lady may later find that she gets a similar kind of pleasure, comfort or relief when she eats or when she smokes a cigarette. When she gets a certain kind of relief that temporarily numbs her pain and scratches that "itch" she can become addicted to that thing that brings relief – be it shopping, porn, cigarettes or gambling. This woman will find it difficult to break this addiction if the issue of emotional deprivation is not addressed. Therefore in order to break the cycle of addiction we have to address and heal the deep-seated pain or issues in order to experience total freedom.

Identifying the root cause of the emotional wound or deprivation

1. Work with a counsellor to identify the root cause of the addiction.
2. Address any wound that resulted from the experience.
3. Address any remaining anger or bitterness issues that were part of the experience.
4. The addict must be allowed to grieve the loss associated with the wound.
5. Create accountability structures for the addict.
6. Prepare the addict for times of vulnerability and attack.
7. Protect the addict against emotional triggers by helping them identify those triggers and choose positive responses beforehand. Remember unhealed wounds raise painful feelings that often result in relapse.
8. Pray and deal with any spiritual issues that resulted from the addiction.
9. Open your heart and spirit to receive and remain in God's unconditional love.

Prayer Points against the Assignment of Drugs

Drugs – Pray against any form of substance abuse against your body i.e. .God's temple e.g. alcohol, smoking, hard drugs, prescription drugs, caffeine, gluttony and eating disorders.

Prayer

Father I receive power over my (insert type of addiction). I break every stronghold of (insert type of addiction) addiction and expel every spirit that is not of God that is at work in my life through this addiction in Jesus name - *Isaiah 49:24*. I declare that sin shall not have dominion over me - *Romans 6: 6*. I ask that You grant me a deep desire to be free of this addiction. I ask that You will help me deal with the addiction from the root that I may be totally and permanently delivered. I pray that You will send me skilled helpers to get and remain free of addiction. Father, also send friends and supporters to help me fight this addiction. I also pray that You will separate me from every association that ties me to this addiction. I declare that the person You have set free, is free indeed - **John 8:36.** This is my portion in Jesus name. Amen.

Scriptures for prayer

John 8:36
Therefore if the Son makes you free, you shall be free indeed.

Romans 6: 6,14
6 knowing this that our old man was crucified with Him, that the body of sin might be done away with, that we should no longer be slaves of sin. 14 For sin shall not have dominion over you, for you are not under law but under grace.

Isaiah 49:24
Shall the prey be taken from the mighty, or the lawful captives of the just be delivered?

1 Corinthians 6:12

All things are lawful for me, but all things are not helpful. All things are lawful for me, but I will not be brought under the power of any.

Philippians 4:13

I can do all this through him who gives me strength.

CHAPTER TWELVE

DIVINATION (WITCHCRAFT AND OCCULT)

The Facts

- It is believed that there are about 400,000 to 3 million practitioners of Wicca in the U.S.[85]
- Some claim Wicca is the fastest growing religion in the U.S.[86]
- Some years ago, 2,500 Satanists were reported to have come together in Pretoria, South Africa to curse marriages.[87]
- The Harry Potter book series sold 400 million copies worldwide and has been translated into 67 languages around the world.
- The Harry Potter film series is said to be the highest grossing film series of all time.

Of 500 Pastors studied and tracked since the 1960s until now,[88]

- 80% of Pastors with occultist surnames failed.
- 60% of Pastors who were converted occultist failed.
- 85% of Pastors whose parents were satanic priests failed.
- 75% of Pastors from polygamous homes failed.
- 9% of Pastors from born-again parents failed.

What is the Occult?

The Occult pertains to magic, astrology, or any system claiming use or knowledge of secret or supernatural powers or agencies. It is beyond the range of ordinary knowledge or understanding; it is mysterious. It involves secrets disclosed or communicated only to the initiated. It means to be hidden from view.

Some Different Operations of the Occult

- Idolatry
- Divination
- Witchcraft

What is Idolatry

Idolatry involves worshipping any God other than God who created the Heaven and earth and making covenants with the devil and his demonic spirits. Idolatry can involve the worship of one's ancestors or angelic beings.

What is Divination?

Divination is the practice of attempting to foretell future events or discover hidden knowledge, by occult or supernatural means. It is

---

[96] http://www.jesus-is- savior.com/False%20Religions/Wicca%20&%20 Witchcraft/teens_and_witchcraft.htm

[97] http://en.wikipedia.org/wiki/Claims_to_be_the_fastest-growing_religion

[98] http://enjoyyourmarriage.com/home/63-book-teasers?start=1

[99] Dr. D. K. Olukoya "When the deliverer needs deliverance"

perception by intuition or instinctive foresight.

Fortune-telling is a type of divination. It is the act or practice of predicting the future.

As in the case of backslidden King Saul, people tend to resort to psychics, séances and mediums in search for answers to their problems. By looking for illegitimate short cuts to long term problems, they want to bypass God's will and His way in order to have things their own way and in their own time. They visit native priests, spiritist churches, false prophets, astrologers and dabble into Eastern mysticism to discern what the future holds for them. Divination is the counterfeit of Biblical prophecy. It is the acquisition of intimate knowledge of the future or unknown by meddling with demons.

Those who dabble into divination want to know the future and are looking for the power to control their own destiny.

"And when Saul inquired of the LORD, the LORD did not answer him, either by dreams or by Urim or by the prophets.
7 Then Saul said to his servants, "Find me a woman who is a medium, that I may go to her and inquire of her." And his servants said to him, "In fact, there is a woman who is a medium at En Dor."
8 So Saul disguised himself and put on other clothes and he went and two men with him; and they came to the woman by night. And he said, "Please conduct a seance for me and bring up for me the one I shall name to you."
9 Then the woman said to him, "Look, you know what Saul has done, how he has cut off the mediums and the spiritists from the land. Why then do you lay a snare for my life, to cause me to die?"
10 And Saul swore to her by the LORD, saying, "As the LORD lives, no punishment shall come upon you for this thing."

11 Then the woman said, "Whom shall I bring up for you?" And he said, "Bring up Samuel for me."

12 When the woman saw Samuel, she cried out with a loud voice. And the woman spoke to Saul, saying, "Why have you deceived me? For you are Saul!"

13 And the king said to her, "Do not be afraid. What did you see?" And the woman said to Saul, "I saw a spirit ascending out of the earth."

14 So he said to her, "What is his form?" And she said, "An old man is coming up and he is covered with a mantle." And Saul perceived that it was Samuel and he stooped with his face to the ground and bowed down.

15 Now Samuel said to Saul, "Why have you disturbed me by bringing me up?" And Saul answered, "I am deeply distressed; for the Philistines make war against me and God has departed from me and does not answer me anymore, neither by prophets nor by dreams. Therefore I have called you, that you may reveal to me what I should do."

16 Then Samuel said: "Why then do you ask me, seeing the LORD has departed from you and has become your enemy?

17 "And the LORD has done for Himself as He spoke by me. For the LORD has torn the kingdom out of your hand and given it to your neighbour, David." (1Samuel 28:6-17)

SOME DIFFERENT FORMS OF DIVINATION

- **Necromancy:** The practice of predicting the future by communicating with the dead.
- **Chiromancy:** divination by use of the palms.
- **Arithmomancy**: Fortune telling by use of numbers.

- **Astrology**
- Crystal balls/gazing
- Use of Ouija boards

What is Witchcraft?

Witchcraft is the illegitimate use of power. It can generally be described as the use of supernatural power outside of God to achieve one's personal agenda and self interest e.g. it is the use of illegitimate powers for the purpose of acquiring money, power, control or even love. Witchcraft is the use of curses, spells or omens to control people or circumstances. It is usually done by the invocation of supernatural forces to assist one personally or to cause harm or to hinder another person's cause. A great Biblical example of this is Balak inviting Balaam to curse God's people in Numbers 22 and 23.

Ancient Witchcraft (Black and White Magic)

Magic is the counterfeit of Biblical miracles. It is man's attempt to perform wonders with the assistance of demonic spirits. Practitioners of witchcraft in the Western world usually distinguish and pride themselves in the decent approach and sophistication of their art, claiming they use their powers only for good and calling it white magic. This is not true because the source of the power is evil and an evil tree cannot bear good fruit.

African Witchcraft (Black Magic, Voodoo and Juju)
According to Rev. Joe Olaiya in his book "Smashing the forces of Evil"; the African witch is more or less a black magic operator.

They are people who are sold out to the devil to work evil wonders, for their own ends. They can assist or afflict, they can destroy or recover. They exercise their dominion by inflicting terror on their communities. The African witch is notable in the use of visible and invisible personalities to effect or execute their plans by sending out an "evil presence". They operate by the enablement of demons and companion spirits with which the witchdoctor, wizard or witch is in league.

"And when they shall say unto you, Seek unto them that <u>have familiar spirits and</u> unto <u>wizards</u> that <u>peep</u> and that <u>mutter</u>: should not a people seek unto their God for the living to the dead?" (Isaiah 8:19)

This operation is a counterfeit operation to the way the Holy Spirit works with and empowers the believer with the nine gifts of the Holy Spirit (tongues, prophecy, word of knowledge and wisdom and working of miracles) for good and God's purpose; they are demonically empowered to do evil by demonic spirits.

SIMON THE SORCERER

"But there was a certain man called Simon, <u>who previously practiced sorcery</u> in the city and <u>astonished the people of Samaria</u>, claiming that he was someone great,

10 to whom <u>they all gave heed, from the least to the greatest</u>, saying, <u>"This man is the great power of God."</u>

11 And <u>they heeded him</u> because <u>he had astonished them with his sorceries for a long time.</u>

12 But when they believed Philip as he preached the things concerning the kingdom of God and the name of Jesus Christ, both men and women were baptized.

13 Then Simon himself also believed; and when he was baptized he continued with Philip and was amazed, seeing the miracles and signs which were done.

14 Now when the apostles who were at Jerusalem heard that Samaria had received the word of God, they sent Peter and John to them,

15 who, when they had come down, prayed for them that they might receive the Holy Spirit.

16 For as yet He had fallen upon none of them. They had only been baptized in the name of the Lord Jesus.

17 Then they laid hands on them and they received the Holy Spirit.

18 And when Simon saw that through the laying on of the apostles' hands the Holy Spirit was given, he offered them money,

19 saying, "Give me this power also, that anyone on whom I lay hands may receive the Holy Spirit."

20 But Peter said to him, "Your money perish with you, because you thought that the gift of God could be purchased with money!

21 "You have neither part nor portion in this matter, for your heart is not right in the sight of God.

22 "Repent therefore of this your wickedness and pray God if perhaps the thought of your heart may be forgiven you.

23 "For I see that you are poisoned by bitterness and bound by iniquity."

24 Then Simon answered and said, "Pray to the Lord for me, that none of the things which you have spoken may come upon me."''
(Acts8:9-24)

In the above passage Simon the former Sorcerer though now converted, sought to buy the power of the Holy Spirit and incurred the wrath and curse of God. Simon did this because buying power and the assistance of spirits was common practice in the world of witchcraft and the occult.

Witchcraft mode of operation

Witchcraft works by the use of demonic powers to cast spells that astonish, mesmerise and hold people spellbound in order to control and influence them for their own selfish purposes.

Rev. Olaiya[89] states that witches can seduce, manipulate their victim's mind or make him take stupid decisions. By co-operation with demons, witches can also influence accidents, destructions, incite conflicts, influence people into errors and torment their victims.

Elymas the Sorcerer

"Now when they had gone through the island to Paphos, they found a certain sorcerer, a false prophet, a Jew whose name was Bar-Jesus,

7 who was with the proconsul, Sergius Paulus, an intelligent man. This man called for Barnabas and Saul and sought to hear the word of God.

8 But Elymas the sorcerer (for so his name is translated) **withstood them, seeking to turn the proconsul away from the faith.**

9 Then Saul, who also is called **Paul, filled with the Holy Spirit,** *looked intently at him*

10 and said, "O full of all deceit and all fraud, you son of the devil, you enemy of all righteousness, will you not **cease perverting the straight ways of the Lord?**

11 "And now, indeed, the hand of the Lord is upon you and **you**

---

[100] Olaiya, P.J.A, Rev., Smashing the forces of evil

__shall be blind, not seeing the sun for a time__." And immediately a dark mist fell on him and he went around seeking someone to lead him by the hand.
12 Then the proconsul believed, when he saw what had been done, being astonished at the teaching of the Lord." (Acts13:6-12)

We see a demonstration in the above scriptures how witchcraft can be used to influence, manipulate and turn people from and even pervert, the ways of the Lord. In both the cases of Simon and Elymas the Sorcerers we see how witchcraft can be used for the control of people's wills (influence). Through the aid of demonic spirits, they can charm people and win their affections, make them do their biddings, dominate their spouses and overpower their wills, emotions and intellect. Just as Christians are supernaturally gifted, Satan has also endowed some people with strange abilities.

WITCHCRAFT POWER OBTAINED THROUGH COVENANTS AND SACRIFICE

These strange abilities are received by initiation or when people enter into demonic covenants and rites with certain deities through sacrifice. The deities promise and give the individual strange powers and abilities in return. Powers often promised include the power to heal, to charm, to overpower others, to have supernatural knowledge and insight and even the power to rule and make decrees and to open barren wombs.

The use of these powers comes with certain strict and deadly conditions. They may require regular sacrifices, the death of loved ones or other deadly penalties for generations to come if their side of the covenant is not kept. Usually, the greater the power that is requested for, the higher the value of the sacrifice that is demanded. Sacrifices can range from chickens and goats to bulls and sometimes human beings depending on the price sought.

*"And when the king of Moab saw that **the battle was too fierce for him**, he took with him seven hundred men who drew swords, to break through to the king of Edom, but they could not.*

*27 Then **he took his eldest son who would have reigned in his place** and **offered him as a burnt offering upon the wall**; and **there was great indignation against Israel. So they departed from him** and returned to their own land."* (1Kings3:26-27)

We see this played out in the battle of Moab against Israel where the King of Moab sacrificed his son in order to defeat Israel and the battle was overturned in his favour. This shows how witchcraft manipulations are used to obtain natural victories.

ANCESTRAL WITCHCRAFT

"Now it happened, as we went to prayer, that a certain slave girl possessed with a spirit of divination met us, who brought her masters much profit by fortune-telling.
17 This girl followed Paul and us and cried out, saying, "These men are the servants of the Most High God, who proclaim to us the way of salvation."
18 And this she did for many days. But Paul, greatly annoyed, turned and said to the spirit, "I command you in the name of Jesus Christ to come out of her." And he came out that very hour.

19 But when her masters saw that their hope of profit was gone, they seized Paul and Silas and dragged them into the marketplace to the authorities." (Acts16:16-19)

We see here how a **spirit of divination** had come to possess and empower the slave girl such that she had the supernatural ability to use fortune-telling to predict people's futures.

""There shall not be found among you anyone who makes his son or his daughter pass through the fire, or one who practices witchcraft, or a soothsayer, or one who interprets omens, or a sorcerer,
11 "or one who conjures spells, or a medium, or a spiritist, or one who calls up the dead.
12 "For all who do these things are an abomination to the LORD and because of these abominations the LORD your God drives them out from before you." (Deuteronomy18:10-12)

Such powers could have come through the initiation of the girl (as seen in the above verse) through the entering of covenants ratified by sacrifices or it could have been passed down from one generation to the other as these covenants are usually made with families for generations to come.

"Now Jacob went out from Beersheba and went toward Haran.
11 So he came to a certain place and stayed there all night, because the sun had set. And he took one of the stones of that place and put it at his head and he lay down in that place to sleep.
12 Then he dreamed and behold, a ladder was set up on the earth and its top reached to heaven; and there the angels of God were ascending and descending on it.
13 And behold, the LORD stood above it and said: "I am the LORD God of Abraham your father and the God of Isaac; the land on

which you *lie I will give to you and your descendants.*

14 *"Also your descendants shall be as the dust of the earth; you shall spread abroad to the west and the east, to the north and the south; and in you and in your seed all the families of the earth shall be blessed.*

15 *"Behold, I am with you and will keep you wherever you go and will bring you back to this land; for I will not leave you until I have done what I have spoken to you."*

16 *Then Jacob awoke from his sleep and said, "Surely the LORD is in this place and I did not know it."*

17 *And he was afraid and said, "How awesome is this place! This is none other than the house of God and this is the gate of heaven!"*

18 *Then Jacob rose early in the morning and took the stone that he had put at his head, set it up as a pillar and poured oil on top of it." (Genesis 28:10-18)*

We see in the above passage how a covenant can be re-enacted and the companion spirits of the deity can be transferred from one generation to another. In this case the covenant God made with Abraham and Isaac gave Jehovah God an entry point to visit Jacob in his dream to re-initiate the same covenant. It also gave an access point to the angels of God to ascend and descend into Jacob's life to empower him for God's purpose.

The same holds true with demonic deities. Since all truth is parallel it means if a person made a covenant with **"Ogun"** (a West African god of war, politics, iron and fire) to secure power to protect him from evil and overpower his enemies in the time of battle and sacrifices were made to ratify the covenant; that same deity can visit the descendants of the same individual in their dream and like the angels, the companion spirits attached to the deity can access the individual's children's lives in another generation or geographical location to empower them for evil. In this case, **"Ogun"** may still visit the grand-children of the same man in their dreams in order to re-invoke the same covenant with them or to give them strange powers and abilities to foresee evil through the supernatural endowment of evil spirits.

"when I call to remembrance <u>the genuine faith</u> that is in you, which dwelt first in <u>your grandmother</u> Lois and <u>your mother</u> Eunice and <u>I am persuaded is in you also.</u>
6 Therefore I remind you <u>to stir up the gift of God which is in you</u> through <u>the laying on of my hands</u>." (*2 Timothy1:5-6*)

If faith can be transferred from one generation to generation, as well as by initiation (as seen in the above verses), then the rights to access demonic mantles and spirits and strange gifts and abilities can be transferred from one generation to another.

THE POWER OF DREAMS AND NAMES

Family lines are very important. If the previous covenant is not wilfully renounced, familial spirits will still try to access anyone in that family line by visiting them in their dreams or in any other way he can gain access into their lives to harass them. This could happen regardless of the fact that the grandchild of a covenanted family has never been to Africa, lives in Chelsea, London, schooled in Oxford and no longer answers to his parents surname **Ogundiya**, but has abbreviated his name for convenience and is now called **John Diya.** Dreams are very important because they can reveal the root cause of certain demonic influences and manipulations (just as Jacob's dream revealed to him that he would benefit because of a covenant God had with his fathers - Genesis 28).

Natural (Dormant) and Functional Witchcraft

People with natural (dormant) witchcraft have been dedicated to these deities from before their birth and inherit strange abilities but have no real awareness of the source. This happens because they were in their father's loins when he made covenants with certain deities.

"Even Levi, who receives tithes, <u>paid tithes through Abraham</u>, so to speak,10 for <u>he was still in the loins of his father</u> when Melchizedek met him." (Hebrews 7:9-10)

They are like dormant terrorist "sleeper cells" that may be called upon and activated sometime. Some are so bad that it seems like the demonic powers take over their consciousness and manifest though their lives.

"Then they brought him to Him. And when he saw Him, immediately <u>the spirit convulsed him</u> and <u>he fell on the ground and wallowed, foaming at the mouth.</u>
 21 So He asked his father, "How long has this been happening to him?" And he said, "<u>From childhood.</u>
 22 "And often <u>he has thrown him both into the fire and into the water to destroy him</u>. But if You can do anything, have compassion on us and help us."" (Mark 9:20)

Invoking Witchcraft in the Ancestry

Always remember that witchcraft is really a "…work of the flesh" (according to Galatians 5:19-22). Just like lying, stealing, sexual immorality, one can be drawn away by one's lust for power and yield to the flesh. The companion (familial) spirits attached to certain deities usually hang around family lines looking for weak, vulnerable and yielded vessels to use.

"But I see another law in my members, warring against the law of my mind and bringing me into captivity to the law of sin which is in my members" (Romans 7:23)

"And do not present your members as instruments of unrighteousness to sin, but present yourselves to God as being alive from the dead and your members as instruments of righteousness to God." (Romans 6:13)

According to Obii Pax-Harry in her book; "Breaking the bonds of Wickedness in the last days", the call to duty for persons bonded to evil, such as ancestral witchcraft is by invocation as opposed to anointing for a commissioned disciple of Christ. These persons bonded to evil are usually located in the spirit realm by witch doctors and caretakers of shrines and other gatekeepers of evil. When the lot falls upon such people to serve their deities, they will unfortunately be located in the spirit if their hearts are not fully yielded to the Lord upon deliverance after becoming born-again. Similar to electronics, they respond to remote controlled signals of their fraternities. These people could then become open doors for demonic altars that allow demonic activities even in churches.

THE CALL TO WITCHCRAFT PRIESTHOOD

To buttress the above points, a certain successful professional lady came to see me asking me to pray for her because she usually had certain demonic visitations and manifestations. On further enquiry I found that her grandfather used to be a very powerful fetish High Priest of a certain tribe in Africa. When he died, the lot fell on her father who was his only child, but he defected and ran away to East Africa. She said anytime she had these demonic manifestations, her mother would inform her that it was her grand-father's demonic priesthood calling her to come to take up his mantle and sit on his throne in order to serve and appease the deity. Of course, she refused to go back to take on the said mantle. Even though she was a believer, she unfortunately did not live a life that was fully yielded to the Lord. A few years later, she began to experience one tragedy after the other as she began to lose one loved one after the other to death; she also lost a lot of money and a number of her prime investments.

WITCHCRAFT FOR HIRE

Those who do not have access to witchcraft powers through initiation or invocation can get it by hiring the services of a wizard, witch, or witch doctor. These people can cast spells, make potions, prepare charms, consult the oracle and interpret omens.

"'Look, a people has come out of Egypt and they cover the face of the earth. Come now, curse them for me; perhaps I shall be able to overpower them and drive them out.'"
12 And God said to Balaam, "You shall not go with them; you shall not curse the people, for they are blessed."
13 So Balaam rose in the morning and said to the princes of Balak, "Go back to your land, for the LORD has refused to give me permission to go with you."
14 And the princes of Moab rose and went to Balak and said, "Balaam refuses to come with us."
15 Then Balak again sent princes, more numerous and more

honourable than they.

16 And they came to Balaam and said to him, "Thus says Balak the son of Zippor: 'Please let nothing hinder you from coming to me;

17 'for I will certainly honour you greatly and I will do whatever you say to me. Therefore please come, curse this people for me.'"

18 Then Balaam answered and said to the servants of Balak, "Though Balak were to give me his house full of silver and gold, I could not go beyond the word of the LORD my God, to do less or more." (Numbers 22:11-18)

WITCHCRAFT CHARMS, AMULETS, CONCOCTIONS AND INCISIONS

When people visit witchdoctors for supernatural power or protection, they are usually given some tools of the trade by which to make contact with the empowering spirit in order to invoke them, cast spells and wrought demonic wonders. Concoctions are made and drunk and blood incisions made to initiate blood covenants of protection and sometimes certain charms are recited by which they make incantations to invoke the demonic powers.

"Likewise, son of man, set your face against the daughters of your people, who prophesy out of their own heart; prophesy against them,

18 "and say, 'Thus says the Lord GOD: "Woe to the women who sew magic charms on their sleeves and make veils for the heads of people of every height to hunt souls! Will you hunt the souls of My people and keep yourselves alive?

19 "And will you profane Me among My people for handfuls of *barley and for pieces of bread, <u>killing people who should not die</u> <u>and</u> keeping people alive who should not live, by your lying to My people who listen to lies?"*

20 'Therefore thus says the Lord GOD: "Behold, <u>I am against your</u> <u>magic charms by which you hunt souls</u> there like birds. I will tear them from your arms and <u>let the souls go,</u> the souls you hunt like birds.

21 "I will <u>also tear off your veils</u> and <u>deliver My people out of your</u> <u>hand and</u> they shall no longer be as prey in your hand. Then you shall know that I am the LORD." (Ezekiel13:17-21)

MODERN WITCHCRAFT; HARRY POTTER ET AL

Witchcraft is operated openly and unashamedly in the Western world. In fact, some witchcraft books are included as part of the curriculum in children's summer school camps and form part of the reading list on the national school curriculum. A whole section in popular bookshops is dedicated to the sale of books on witchcraft, Satanism, astrology and eastern mysticism and other mystical works.

*"Also, many of those who had **practiced magic** brought **their books** together and burned them in the sight of all. And **they counted up** **the value of them** and **it totalled fifty thousand pieces of silver**.*
So the word of the Lord grew mightily and prevailed." (Acts19:19-20)

The other day, I saw a book titled "Witchcraft made easy" on the shelf in a branch of perhaps the largest bookshop chain in the U.K and an article on "How to cast a spell and make love portions" on the pages of a very popular newspaper.

Harry Potter, a book about a boy wizard and his friends openly practising witchcraft and casting spells has become a popular phenomenon amongst children the world over, provoking a worldwide witchcraft revival. Harry Potter is a series of seven fantasy novels written by the British author J. K. Rowling. The books chronicle the adventures of the adolescent wizard Harry Potter and his best friends Ron Weasley and Hermione Granger, all of whom are students at Hogwarts School of Witchcraft and Wizardry. The main story concerns Harry's quandary involving the evil wizard Lord Voldemort, who killed Harry's parents in his quest to conquer the wizarding world and subjugate non-magical people (Muggles).

The same book has sold over 400 million copies worldwide and has been translated into 67 languages around the world. The Harry Potter film series is said to be the highest grossing film series of all time. This book and films have held the whole world literally spellbound.

As of March 2010, when its latest world billionaires list was published, Forbes estimated Rowling's net worth to be $1 billion.[7]The 2008 Sunday Times Rich List estimated Rowling's fortune at £560 million ($798 million), ranking her as the twelfth richest woman in Great Britain. Forbes ranked Rowling as the forty-eighth most powerful celebrity of 2007.[90]

These days, there are so many witchcraft-related movies and TV series that feature on our screens, such as Buffy the Teenage Vampire, Sabrina the Witch, Bewitched, Charmed, Enchanted, Teenage Witches and a number of series relating to vampires. Video games such as Warcraft and Pokémon (Pocket monster) are now the preferred toys for many children. Evil it seems is now an acceptable entertainment and leisure option.

"O foolish Galatians! Who has <u>bewitched you</u> that you should <u>not obey the truth</u>, before whose eyes Jesus Christ was clearly portrayed among you as crucified?" Galatians 3:1

Is a whole generation being seduced and lulled into witchcraft? Is this a Witchcraft revival? Where is the power of the church to reverse this trend like we saw in the scripture above? (Acts19:19-20)

Witchcraft today is painted as harmless fun and a force for good. Regardless of how it is packaged, branded and sold, it does not take away its lethal nature and the fact that it is an abomination to the Lord. Dabbling into witchcraft at any level is a sin, with extremely grave consequences.

CONTEMPORARY WITCHCRAFT

Another form of Witchcraft is the use of control, intimidation, manipulation and domination to achieve one's personal agenda. We see this scenario play out in the scripture that follows.

"So Ahab went into his house <u>sullen and displeased</u> because of the word which Naboth the Jezreelite had spoken to him; for he had said, "I will not give you the inheritance of my fathers." And he lay down on his bed and turned away his face and would eat no food.
5 But Jezebel his wife came to him and said to him, "Why is your spirit so sullen that you eat no food?"
6 He said to her, "Because I spoke to Naboth the Jezreelite and said to him, 'Give me your vineyard for money; or else, if it pleases you, I will give you another vineyard for it.' And he answered, 'I

will not give you my vineyard.'"

7 Then Jezebel his wife said to him, <u>"You now exercise authority</u> <u>over Israel!</u> Arise, eat food and let your heart be cheerful; I will give you the vineyard of Naboth the Jezreelite."

8 And <u>she wrote letters in Ahab's name, sealed them with his seal</u> <u>and </u>sent the letters to the elders and the nobles who were dwelling in the city with Naboth.

9 She wrote in the letters, saying<u>, Proclaim a fast and </u>seat Naboth with high honour among the people;

10 and seat two men, scoundrels, <u>before him to bear witness</u> <u>against him, saying, "You have blasphemed God and the king."</u> <u>Then take him out and stone him, that he may die.</u>

11 So the men of his city, the elders and nobles who were inhabitants of his city, <u>did as Jezebel had sent to them, as it was</u> <u>written in the letters which she had sent to them.</u>

12 They proclaimed a fast and seated Naboth with high honour among the people.

13 And two men, scoundrels, came in and sat before him; and the scoundrels witnessed against him, against Naboth, in the presence of the people, saying, "Naboth has blasphemed God and the king!" Then they took him outside the city and stoned him with stones, so that he died.

14 Then they sent to Jezebel, saying, "Naboth has been stoned and is dead."

15 And it came to pass, when Jezebel heard that Naboth had been stoned and was dead, that Jezebel said to Ahab, <u>"Arise, take</u> <u>possession of the vineyard of Naboth the Jezreelite, which he</u> <u>refused to give you for money; for Naboth is not alive, but dead."</u>

16 So it was, when Ahab heard that Naboth was dead, that Ahab got up and went down to take possession of the vineyard of Naboth the Jezreelite." (1 Kings21:4-16)

THE CONSEQUENCES OF DABBLING INTO DARK POWERS

Perhaps the saddest consequence of this is that it opens the door for satanic interference for generations into a family line.

THE SINS OF THE FATHERS

""You shall have <u>no other gods before Me.</u>
4 "You shall not make for yourself <u>a carved image</u>, or any likeness of anything that is in heaven above, or that is in the earth beneath, or that is in the water under the earth; 5you shall not bow down to them nor serve them. For I, the LORD your God, am a jealous God, <u>visiting</u> the <u>iniquity</u> of the fathers on the children to <u>the third</u> and <u>fourth generations</u> of those who hate Me," (Exodus 20:4, 5)

Four Generations above include 30 different people who might have worshipped idols or dabbled into the occult.

30 people= 2 Parents + 4 Grand Parents + 8 Great Grand parents + 16 Great, Great Grandparents.

If any of these dabbled into such abominable practices then their descendants four generations down become candidates for the consequences of the curse.

THE CURSES OF IDOLATRY

According to Mosy Madugba in his book, "Dealing with evil foundations", there are many and severe consequences for dabbling into idolatry and evil powers.

"'<u>Cursed</u> is the one who <u>makes a carved or moulded image</u>, an

abomination to the LORD, the work of the hands of the craftsman and _sets it up in secret.'_ And all the people shall answer and say, 'Amen!'"(Deuteronomy 27:15)

Here are a few of these curses as outlined in scripture.

IT INVITES UNTIMELY AND VIOLENT DEATHS AND MISCARRIAGES INTO THE FAMILY LINE.

_"As for Ephraim, their glory shall fly away like a bird-n_o birth, no pregnancy and no conception!_
 12 Though they bring up their children, yet I will bereave them to the last man. Yes, woe to them when I depart from them!
 13 Just as I saw Ephraim like Tyre, planted in a pleasant place, So Ephraim will bring out his children to the murderer."
 14 Give them, O LORD-What will You give? Give them a miscarrying womb and dry breasts!
 15 "All their wickedness is in Gilgal, for there I hated them. Because of the evil of their deeds I will drive them from My house; I will love them no more. All their princes are rebellious.
 16 Ephraim is stricken, Their root is dried up; They shall bear no fruit. Yes, were they to bear children, I would kill the darlings of their womb."" (Hosea 9:11-16)_

IT CAUSES POVERTY, VIOLENCE, ROBBERY, DROUGHT AND FAMINE.

"A sword is against their horses, against their chariots and against all the mixed peoples who are in her midst; and they will become *like women. A sword is <u>against her treasures and they will be robbed.</u>*

38 <u>A drought</u> is against her waters and they <u>will be dried up</u>. For it is <u>the land of carved images</u> and they are <u>insane with their idols</u>." (*Jeremiah 50:38*)

IT GIVES RISE TO NATURAL DISASTERS... EARTHQUAKES, HURRICANES, VOLCANIC ERUPTIONS.

"4 <u>You shall be brought down</u>, you shall speak out of the ground; your speech shall be low, out of the dust; your voice shall be like a medium's, out of the ground; and your speech shall whisper out of the dust.

5 "Moreover the multitude of your foes shall be like fine dust and the multitude of the terrible ones Like chaff that passes away; Yes, it shall be <u>in an instant, suddenly.</u>

6 You will be punished by the LORD of hosts with <u>thunder</u> and <u>earthquake</u> and great noise, <u>with storm</u> and <u>tempest</u> and the <u>flame of devouring fire</u>." (*Isaiah29:6*)

IT BRINGS A MULTIPLICITY OF SORROWS.

"Their <u>sorrows</u> shall be <u>multiplied</u> who hasten <u>after another god;</u> their drink offerings of blood I will not offer, nor take up their names on my lips." (*Psalm16:4*)

IT LEADS TO BACKWARDNESS (RETROGRESSION) AND A LACK OF PROGRESS.

"They shall be <u>turned back</u>, they shall <u>be greatly ashamed</u>, who trust in carved images, who say to the moulded images, 'You are our gods.'" (Isaiah42:17)

IT BRINGS PEOPLE INTO SERVITUDE, OPPRESSION AND BONDAGE.

"36 They <u>served their idols</u>, which became a <u>snare to them.</u>
37 They even sacrificed their sons and their daughters to demons,
38 And shed innocent blood, the blood of their sons and daughters, whom they sacrificed to the idols of Canaan; and the land was polluted, with blood.
39 Thus they were defiled by their own works and played the harlot by their own deeds.
40 Therefore the wrath of the LORD was kindled against His people, So that He abhorred His own inheritance.
41 And <u>He gave them into the hand of the Gentiles</u> and those <u>who hated them ruled over them.</u>
42 Their <u>enemies also oppressed them</u> and they were brought into subjection under their hand." (Psalm106:35-43)

IT BRINGS ABOUT CONFUSION, SHAME AND DISGRACE.

"They shall be <u>ashamed</u> And also <u>disgraced,</u> all of them; they shall go <u>in confusion</u> together, who are makers of idols." (Isaiah 45:16)

Needless to say, this is one issue that every individual must do all in their power to cut off all involvement in. It will require intense prayer, fasting and frequent renunciation of evil ties and the declaration of the lordship of the Lord Jesus Christ in the life of the individual.

PRAYER POINT AGAINST THE ASSIGNMENT OF DIVINATION

Divination – Pray against the effect and or impact of the spirit of witchcraft, divination, the occult, astrology and cults.

PRAYER

Father I repent of any sin or covenant of idolatry entered into by me or my forbears, I renounce every such sin and covenant before the Lord and I withdraw my allegiance from the pledges, vows and commitments made to any strange spirits by my forbears. I command every token exchanged on my behalf to be destroyed.
By the Blood of Jesus, I silence the declarations of these evil covenants and discharge and de-robe every satanic priest that watch over these altars, I terminate their assignments, cut them off from their source of power and bind the strongman that empowers that covenant in the name of Jesus.

I receive power from the Holy Spirit to overcome any witchcraft, divination or ancestral spirits hovering over my life. I break every stronghold of any demonic origin and expel every spirit that is not of God that is at work in my life through any covenant entered into by myself or by my forbears in Jesus name.

I renounce every covenant made by myself or my forbears; I seal every crack or access points through which ancestral spirits might want to gain access to my life, family or enterprise. I declare them illegal and sealed by the blood of Jesus.

I revoke and nullify the power of every curse, or token sent or spoken against me to destroy or cause afflictions as a result of past covenants or recent evil conspiracies.

According to that which is written in Isaiah54:17, I declare that every weapon (Curse, Invocation, Token, etc) formed or fashioned against me shall fail and not prosper in its cause and every evil tongue that rises up against me is condemned in Jesus name.

Every device of wickedness formed and launched against my life and members of my family, I nullify by the blood of Jesus.

I frustrate any enchantment and divination used against me and I turn their wisdom and knowledge into foolishness (Isaiah 44:25-26) in the name of Jesus.

I destroy every evil device planted in my system knowingly or unknowingly and I pull them up from the root and I decree and declare that I am totally and permanently delivered from their effects.

The blood of Jesus nullifies Satan's legal access to me, I am covered with the blood of Jesus, therefore I cannot be touched by any form wickedness.

I stop all assailants, fiery darts and arrows launched against me by the power in the blood of Jesus. I declare that no evil shall come near my dwelling place.

I declare that the person that Jesus has set free, is free indeed - **John 8:36.** This is my portion in Jesus name. Amen.

SCRIPTURES FOR PRAYER

Numbers 23:23
For there is no sorcery against Jacob, nor any divination against Israel. It now must be said of Jacob and of Israel, 'Oh, what God has done!'

Isaiah 54:17
No weapon formed against you shall prosper, and every tongue which rises against you in judgment you shall condemn. This is the heritage of the servants of the LORD, and their righteousness is from Me," Says the LORD.

Isaiah44:25-26
"Who frustrates the signs of the babblers, and drives diviners mad; Who turns wise men backward, And makes their knowledge foolishness;
26 Who confirms the word of His servant, And performs the counsel of His messengers; Who says to Jerusalem, 'You shall be inhabited,' To the cities of Judah, 'You shall be built,' And I will raise up her waste places;"

Isaiah47:11-14
"11 Therefore evil shall come upon you; You shall not know from where it arises. And trouble shall fall upon you; you will not be able to put it off. And desolation shall come upon you suddenly, which you shall not know.
12 "Stand now with your enchantments and the multitude of your sorceries, In which you have laboured from your youth-Perhaps

you will be able to profit, Perhaps you will prevail.

13 You are wearied in the multitude of your counsels; Let now the astrologers, the stargazers, and the monthly prognosticators Stand up and save you from what shall come upon you.

14 Behold, they shall be as stubble, the fire shall burn them; they shall not deliver themselves From the power of the flame; It shall not be a coal to be warmed by, Nor a fire to sit before!"

Ezekiel 13:6-9

"3 Surely He shall deliver you from the snare of the fowler and from the perilous pestilence.

4 He shall cover you with His feathers, and under His wings you shall take refuge; His truth shall be your shield and buckler.

5 You shall not be afraid of the terror by night, Nor of the arrow that flies by day,

6 Nor of the pestilence that walks in darkness, Nor of the destruction that lays waste at noonday.

7 A thousand may fall at your side, and ten thousand at your right hand; but it shall not come near you.

8 Only with your eyes shall you look, and see the reward of the wicked."- Psalm91:3-8

"6 "They have envisioned futility and false divination, saying, 'Thus says the LORD!' But the LORD has not sent them; yet they hope that the word may be confirmed.

7 "Have you not seen a futile vision, and have you not spoken false divination? You say, 'The LORD says,' but I have not spoken."

8 Therefore thus says the Lord GOD: "Because you have spoken nonsense and envisioned lies, therefore I am indeed against you," says the Lord GOD.

9 "My hand will be against the prophets who envision futility and

who divine lies; they shall not be in the assembly of My people, nor be written in the record of the house of Israel, nor shall they enter into the land of Israel. Then you shall know that I am the Lord GOD."-

""and say, 'thus says the Lord GOD: "Woe to the women who sew magic charms on their sleeves and make veils for the heads of people of every height to hunt souls! Will you hunt the souls of My people, and keep yourselves alive?

Ezekiel 13:18-23

19 "And will you profane Me among My people for handfuls of barley and for pieces of bread, killing people who should not die, and keeping people alive who should not live, by your lying to My people who listen to lies?"

20 'therefore thus says the Lord GOD: "Behold, I am against your magic charms by which you hunt souls there like birds. I will tear them from your arms, and let the souls go, the souls you hunt like birds.

21 "I will also tear off your veils and deliver My people out of your hand, and they shall no longer be as prey in your hand. Then you shall know that I am the LORD.

22 "Because with lies you have made the heart of the righteous sad, whom I have not made sad; and you have strengthened the hands of the wicked, so that he does not turn from his wicked way to save his life.

23 "Therefore you shall no longer envision futility nor practice divination; for I will deliver My people out of your hand, and you shall know that I am the LORD."""-

Chapter Thirteen

Conclusion

Dominion over all the Power of the enemy

"And Jesus summoned to Him His twelve disciples and <u>gave them power</u> and authority <u>over unclean spirits</u>, to <u>drive them out</u> and to <u>cure all kinds of disease</u> and all kinds of weakness and infirmity." Matthew 10:10

Now that we are aware of the 12 commonest devices Satan has formed and fashioned against this generation, what should our reaction be?

Do not be afraid!

""<u>No man</u> shall be able to stand before you all the days of your life; as I was with Moses, <u>so I will be with you</u>. I will not leave you nor forsake you.

6 "Be strong and of good courage, for to this people you shall divide as an inheritance the land which I swore to their fathers to give them.

7 "Only be strong and very courageous, that you may observe to do according to all the law which Moses My servant commanded you; do not turn from it to the right hand or to the left, that you may prosper wherever you go." Joshua1:5-7

It is important for you to know that God is also aware and that He has made provision for your protection. He has promised not to leave us or forsake us and in as much as we do not leave Him or forsake Him, "No man (or demon shall be able to stand before you all the days of your life; … "If you ever stray, return quickly and repent so that you are not open to attack.

WE HAVE SUPERIOR POWER!

Now that you know your enemy and his plans and strategies, you must be careful not to focus on him, his devices and his past victories with others, but rather focus on Jesus, what He has done for you on the Cross and what He will do for you in the day of trouble. In reality, the enemy is really afraid of us.

"11 Therefore the heart of the king of Syria was greatly troubled by this thing; and he called his servants and said to them, "Will you not show me which of us is for the king of Israel?"

12 And one of his servants said, "None, my lord, O king; but Elisha, the prophet who is in Israel, tells the king of Israel the words that you speak in your bedroom."

13 So he said, "Go and see where he is, that I may send and get him." And it was told him, saying, "Surely he is in Dothan."

14 Therefore he sent horses and chariots and a great army there and they came by night and surrounded the city.

15 And when the servant of the man of God arose early and went out, there was an army, surrounding the city with horses and chariots. And his servant said to him, "Alas, my master! What shall we do?"

16 So he answered, "Do not fear, for those who are with us are more than those who are with them."

17 And Elisha prayed and said, "LORD, I pray, open his eyes that he may see." Then the LORD opened the eyes of the young man and he saw. And behold, the mountain was full of horses and chariots of fire all around Elisha.

18 So when the Syrians came down to him, Elisha prayed to the LORD and said, "Strike this people, I pray, with blindness." -And He struck them with blindness according to the word of Elisha."
2Kings 6:11-18

The above passage shows that not only will God protect in the day of evil, He will prepare us for what is to come by giving us prophetic insight into the enemy's plans, so we can prepare in advance. Also, if and when the enemy comes, God assures us that those who are for us outnumber those who are against us, so we should be rest assured in His protective power.

ALWAYS WEAR YOUR PROTECTIVE ARMOUR!

Whatever you do, you must be aware that you are in a continuous warfare and that life is not a funfair. Those who do not live with that mindset can suffer many casualties.

With this in mind, recognise that there is no demilitarised zone and therefore you must keep your spiritual armour on at all times and ensure there is no opening in your armour due to sin or negligence. Satanic forces are always looking to infiltrate and penetrate our defences through sin and other means but you must be watchful.

"Finally, my brethren, be strong in the Lord and in the power of His might.
11 Put on the whole armour of God, that you may be able to stand against the wiles of the devil.
12 For we do not wrestle against flesh and blood, but against principalities, against powers, against the rulers of the darkness of this age, against spiritual hosts of wickedness in the heavenly places.
13 Therefore take up the whole armour of God that you may be able to withstand in the evil day and having done all, to stand.
14 Stand therefore, having girded your waist with truth, having put on the breastplate of righteousness,
15 and having shod your feet with the preparation of the gospel of peace;
16 above all, taking the shield of faith with which you will be able to quench all the fiery darts of the wicked one.
17 And take the helmet of salvation and the sword of the Spirit, which is the word of God;
18 praying always with all prayer and supplication in the Spirit, being watchful to this end with all perseverance and supplication for all the saints." Ephesians 6:10-18

With the above precautions you are well protected against the onslaughts of the evil one. Now, let's look in more detail below about how to exercise the dominion we have in Christ.

TAKING AUTHORITY AND WALKING IN DOMINION

"And Jesus summoned to Him His twelve disciples and gave them power and authority over unclean spirits, to drive them out and to cure all kinds of disease and all kinds of weakness and infirmity."
Matt. 10:10

Jesus did not only make provision for our protection He also made provision for His Kingdom advancement and opportunities for us to take back what the enemy might have stolen from us.

Empowerment: "He gave them Power over ..."

THE BEGINNING OF SPIRITUAL EMPOWERMENT

10 And immediately, coming up from the water, He saw the heavens parting and the Spirit descending upon Him like a dove. Mark 1:10

The above shows Jesus received the empowerment of the Spirit. His Spiritual Empowerment gave Him authority to cast out demonic spirits. If Jesus needed it, we need the same to enjoy the same Dominion as seen below.

"And they were astonished at His teaching, for He taught them as one having authority and not as the scribes.
23 Now there was a man in their synagogue with an unclean spirit. And he cried out,

24 saying, "Let us alone! What have we to do with You, Jesus of
Nazareth? Did You come to destroy us? I know who You are the
Holy One of God!"
25 But Jesus rebuked him, saying, "Be quiet and come out of him!"
26 And when the unclean spirit had convulsed him and cried out
with a loud voice, he came out of him.
27 Then they were all amazed, so that they questioned among
themselves, saying, "What is this? What new doctrine is this? For
with authority He commands even the unclean spirits and they obey
Him."
28 And immediately His fame spread throughout all the region
around Galilee." Mark1:22-28

DAILY SPIRITUAL EMPOWERMENT

He did not depend on His initial empowerment alone but went to
the Father continually for daily empowerment as seen below.

Now in the morning, having risen a long while before daylight, He
went out and departed to a solitary place; and there He prayed.
Mark1:35

Liberation: Power ..._over unclean spirits, to drive them out_

We have power over unclean spirits. The power is given to enable
us to expel any evil spirit or demonic assignments in our lives or
those tormenting the lives of others. As Jesus was empowered by
the Spirit and then went out to set the captives free; we have also
been empowered to do the same by the same Spirit.

""The Spirit of the LORD is upon Me, because He has anointed me
to preach the gospel to the poor; He has sent me to heal the broken-

hearted, <u>to proclaim liberty to the captives</u> and recovery of sight to the blind, <u>to set at liberty those who are oppressed;</u>
19 to proclaim the acceptable year of the LORD."" Luke4:18-19

You can take authority right now and begin to name and command spirits to leave your life and that of those dear to you, in Jesus name.

Restoration: Power - to <u>heal all kinds of disease</u> and kinds of weakness and infirmity…

Even after these destructive elements have been cast out, a restorative work of healing needs to take place. For example, the healing of hearts and the marriage after the spirit of divorce has been cast out or the healing of a broken heart and the restoration of trust after a spirit of defilement has been cast out. Likewise, restoration means the healing of relationships in the home after a spirit of drugs (addictions) has been cast out and the healing of the emotions and restoration of a renewed self-image after the spirit of dejection has been cast out.

Casting out a demon could happen in a moment but healing and restoration may require time, effort, patience and sometimes money.

"Then Jesus answered and said: "A certain man went down from Jerusalem to Jericho and <u>fell among thieves</u>, who <u>stripped him </u>of his clothing, <u>wounded him</u> and departed, <u>leaving him half dead.</u>
31 "Now by chance a certain priest came down that road. And when he saw him, he passed by on the other side.
32 "Likewise a Levite, when he arrived at the place, came and looked and passed by on the other side.
33 "But a certain Samaritan, as he journeyed, came where he was. And when <u>he saw him, he had compassion</u>.
34 "So he went to him and <u>bandaged his wounds, pouring on oil</u>

and wine; and he set him on his own animal, <u>brought him to an inn</u>
<u>and took care of him.</u>
 35 "On the next day, when he departed, he took out two denarii,
gave them to the innkeeper and said to him, <u>'Take care of him; and</u>
<u>whatever more you spend, when I come again, I will repay you.</u>'
 36 "So which of these three do you think was neighbour to him who
fell among the thieves?"" Luke10:30-36

DAMAGED BUT NOT DESTROYED

The above passage further confirms that the devil, the thief, comes to steal, kill and to destroy; and that even if the demons are cast out before the assignment to destroy is accomplished, serious damage might already have been done.

In the story above, the thieves had left but the man had been left for dead, stripped of his clothes and goods and wounded. This is how many people are left after the assigned demons have been cast out and they usually require a season of healing, restoration and rehabilitation. This can take the form of medical help, financial aid, accommodation, counselling, therapy, prayer, a safe place, fellowship, friendship, support and hope for the future.

Other useful resources for gaining and maintaining your deliverance are

Diagnostic tool, Demonic Profiling or Consultation
To identify personal, familial and generational patterns or traits.
Reading Books and Resources
That relate to the areas where you require help. In this way you can assess the skill and experience of those in the know in that area to gain victory.

Spiritual Root Analysis

To identify the spiritual roots of some problems you are experiencing.

Deep Rooted Ministry Retreat

A weekend or days dedicated to identifying the roots of problems and dealing with it in prayer.

Referrals

Making contact with someone experienced in the relevant field to seek solutions to the problem e.g. a counsellor for dejection and depression problems, health professionals for medical problems such as disease or addiction, a financial advisor on debt or a deliverance minister for problems related to the occult.

MAINTAINING THE KEYS TO DOMINION

Last but not least, there are some key personal disciplines that you must develop if you are to get and maintain your deliverance.

The Word

"8 "This Book of the Law shall not depart from your mouth, but you shall <u>meditate on it day and night,</u> that you may observe to do according to all that is written in it. For then you will make your way prosperous and then you will have good success.

9 "Have I not commanded you? Be strong and of good courage; do not be afraid, nor be dismayed, for the LORD your God is with you wherever you go."" Joshua1:8-9

The Word of God is our ultimate key to dominion and our knowledge and practice of it will save us from destruction. Jesus knew the scriptures and quoted it when the devil attacked him.

"Direct my steps by Your word and let no iniquity have dominion over me." Ps119:133

Watchfulness (Revelation)

"Watch and pray, lest you enter into temptation. The spirit indeed is willing, but the flesh is weak." Matthew 26:41

Jesus admonishes us to watch and pray so we do not enter or fall into temptations. This implies that certain disasters can be averted by being spiritually alert to the Spirit's warnings and promptings. We see an example of this when Jesus warned Peter that He had seen **the spirit of deception** overpower him.

"31 And the Lord said, "Simon, Simon! Indeed, Satan has asked for you, that he may sift you as wheat.

32 "But I have prayed for you, that your faith should not fail; and when you have returned to Me, strengthen your brethren."

33 But he said to Him, "Lord, I am ready to go with You, both to prison and to death."

34 Then He said, "I tell you, Peter, the rooster shall not crow this day before you will deny three times that you know Me.""
Luke22:30-34

Unfortunately Peter didn't respond appropriately, he was overconfident and thought he couldn't fall into sin. The right response would have been to pray to be strengthened not to fail at the time of testing and to prepare to stand.

God reveals things in dreams, visions and through prophecy so we can avert it through prayer.

Prayer

The power of prayer to defeat the enemy's plans and forces cannot be over emphasised. Sometimes, certain problems may seem to defy every solution applied but at such times we can fortify our spiritual power by intensifying our prayers with a season of fasting as Jesus indicated in the scripture below.

"21 So He asked his father, "How long has this been happening to him?" And he said, "From childhood.

22 "And often he has thrown him both into the fire and into the water to destroy him. But if You can do anything, have compassion on us and help us."

23 Jesus said to him, "If you can believe, all things are possible to him who believes."

24 Immediately the father of the child cried out and said with tears, "Lord, I believe; help my unbelief!"

25 When Jesus saw that the people came running together, He rebuked the unclean spirit, saying to it, "Deaf and dumb spirit, I command you, come out of him and enter him no more!"

26 Then the spirit cried out, convulsed him greatly and came out of him. And he became as one dead, so that many said, "He is dead."

27 But Jesus took him by the hand and lifted him up and he arose.

28 And when He had come into the house, His disciples asked Him privately, "Why could we not cast it out?"

29 So He said to them, "This kind can come out by nothing but prayer and fasting."" Mark9:21-29

Deliverance

Some but not every case may require some kind of external spiritual intervention such as deliverance. In a session of deliverance, someone with the anointing and expertise in the area of deliverance is called upon to help break a curse or expel a stubborn spirit. It is worth noting though that many times, deliverance will come through the first three keys outlined above.

"Then Jesus said to those Jews who believed Him, "If you <u>abide in My word</u>, you are My disciples indeed.
32 "And you shall know the truth and the <u>truth shall make you free.</u>"" John 8:32, 33

My prayer is that as you take heed to the truths you have learned and apply the keys to dominion outlined, you will experience breakthroughs in every single area of your life.

Remain blessed.

BIBLIOGRAPHY

[1] Matthew 12:25

[2] Ephesians 6:12

[3] 2 Corinthians 2:11 AMP

[4] Proverbs 20:18

[5] Tzu, Sun, (2008) *The Art of War* (Wilder Publications)

[6] Luke 11:22

[7] Exodus 1:15-22

[8] Matthew 2:16

[9] Ibojie, Joe Dr., (2006), *How to live the supernatural life in the here and now* (Destiny Image)

[10] Eckhardt, John Apostle, (1920) *Identifying and Breaking Curses* (Whitaker House)

[11] Eckhardt, John Apostle, (1920) *Identifying and Breaking Curses* (Whitaker House)

[12] Wikipedia, Lincoln-Kennedy coincidences urban legend, http://en.wikipedia.org/wiki/Lincoln-Kennedy_coincidences_urban_legend

[13] Wikipedia

[14] World Health Organisation WHO report.

[15] World Health Organisation WHO report http://www.who.int/mediacentre/factsheets/fs297/en/

[16] World Health Organisation WHO report http://www.who.int/mediacentre/factsheets/fs297/en/

[17] World Health Organisation WHO report http://www.who.int/mediacentre/factsheets/fs297/en/

[18] World Health Organisation WHO report. www.who.int/entity/mediacentre/factsheets/fs297/en/

[19] 2 Peter3:9

[20] Hebrews 9:27

[21] Wikipedia: http://en.wikipedia.org/wiki/HIV

[22] World Health Organisation WHO report. http://www.who.int/dietphysicalactivity/en/

[23] Wikipedia http://en.wikipedia.org/wiki/HIV

[24] World Health Organisation WHO report. http://en.wikipedia.org/wiki/Cancer

[25] John 10:10

[26] Leviticus 13

[27] Leviticus 19:14

[28] World Health Organisation WHO report http://www.who.int/mediacentre/factsheets/fs297/en/

[29] http://www.creditaction.org.uk/debt-statistics/2010/august-2010.html

[30] Peter Meadows, (2003) The Rich thinking about the Worlds poor, Authentic Lifestyle

[31] London, H.B. Jr., (2003) *Pastors at Greater Risk,* Gospel Light Publications

[32] Williams, Jessica, (2007) *50 facts that should change the world,* Icon Books

[33] London, H.B. Jr., (2003) *Pastors at Greater Risk,* Gospel Light Publications

[34] London, H.B. Jr., (2003) *Pastors at Greater Risk,* Gospel Light Publications

[35] Professor Francis and Dr. Kane

[36] Marc Europe and Agape UK

[37] Willard Harley Jr., *Women and Infidelity,* (article) www.marriagebuilders.com

[38] London, H.B. Jr., (2003) *Pastors at Greater Risk,* Gospel Light Publications

[39] London, H.B. Jr., (2003) *Pastors at Greater Risk,* Gospel Light Publications

[40] London, H.B. Jr., (2003) *Pastors at Greater Risk,* Gospel Light Publications

[41] London, H.B. Jr., (2003) *Pastors at Greater Risk,* Gospel Light Publications

[42] Walsh, James, *How to get a quickie-divorce* (article) www.articlesbase.com

[43] Common causes and reasons for divorce (article) www.buzzle.com

[44] Common causes and reasons for divorce (article) www.buzzle.com

45 Common causes and reasons for divorce (article) www.buzzle.com

46 Stringer, Doug, (1995) *The Fatherless generation: Hope for a Generation in Search of Identity*, Destiny Image

47 Stringer, Doug, (1995) *The Fatherless generation: Hope for a Generation in Search of Identity*, Destiny Image

48 London, H.B. Jr., (2003) *Pastors at Greater Risk*, Gospel Light Publications

49 London, H.B. Jr., (2003) *Pastors at Greater Risk*, Gospel Light Publications

50 http://sweetcardomom.wordpress.com/tag/absent-fathers/

51 Schmierer, Don, (2005) *An Ounce of Prevention: Preventing the Homosexual Condition in Today's Youth*, Promise Pub Co

52 Nicholi, Armand M. Dr., *Changes in the American Family*. Family Research Council, nd.

53 http://smallchurch.com/resources/statistics/

54 http://en.wikipedia.org/wiki/Self_image

55 http://en.wikipedia.org/wiki/Self-esteem_instability

56 Bevere, Lisa (1998). *You are not what you weigh: Escaping the lie and living the truth*. Lake Mary, FL: Creation House.

57 Adams, Shelley, Signs of Low Self-Esteem in Women - http://www.ehow.com/about_5075430_signs-low-selfesteem-women.html

50 Baumeister, R. F., (1997). *Evil: Inside human violence and cruelty*. New York: W.H. Freeman., 1997)

59 Hudson et al. The prevalence and correlates of eating disorders in the National Comorbidity Survey Replication.[Biological Psychiatry. 2007 Feb 1;61(3)348-58 PMID 16815322]

60 http://en.wikipedia.org/wiki/Self-esteem_instability

61 Willard Harley Jr., *Women and Infidelity*, (article) www.marriagebuilders.com

62 London, H.B. Jr., (2003) *Pastors at Greater Risk*, Gospel Light Publications

63 Fola-Alade, Sola, Dr., (2003) *So, Who Do You Really Think You Are? How to Heal the Wounds of the Past and Reveal the Real You*. Vision Media

64 Fola-Alade, Sola, Dr., (2003) *So, Who Do You Really Think You Are? How to Heal the Wounds of the Past and Reveal the Real You*. Vision Media

[65] http://en.wikipedia.org/wiki/Eating_disorder

[66] Fola-Alade, Sola, Dr., (2003) *So, Who Do You Really Think You Are? How to Heal the Wounds of the Past and Reveal the Real You.* Vision Media

[67] http://www.promises.com/depression-anxiety.php

[68] www.ecounseling.com/online_counseling/15-depression

[69] http://www.womens-menopause-health.com/Depression/depress_statistics.htm

[70] http://www.namigc.org/content/fact_sheets/generalInfo/PublicAction/web-information-for-writers-on-mi-0304.htm

[71] http://www.benbest.com/lifeext/causes.html

[72] http://www.teensuicidestatistics.com/

[73] http://www.netdoctor.co.uk/diseases/depression/classification_000001.htm

[74] Clinton, Tim, Dr. & Hawkins, Ron, Dr., (2009) *The Quick reference Guide to Biblical Counselling*, Baker Books

[75] Stress and Depression from www.allaboutdepression.com

[76] http://www.nhs.uk/Conditions/Depression/Pages/Symptoms.aspx

[77] http://www.truthaboutdeception.com/lying-and-deception/how- often-lovers-lie/experiments.html

[78] http://www.preventionaction.org/research/liars-learned-lies-%E2%80%93-and-statistics

[79] http://www.preventionaction.org/research/liars-learned-lies-%E2%80%93-and-statistics

[80] http://www.truthaboutdeception.com/lying-and-deception/how-often-lovers lie/experiments.html

[81] This paragraph is an adapted summary of "Learning to Lie" by Po Bronson in New York Magazine, February 10, 2008

[82] http://en.wikipedia.org/wiki/Deception

[83] This survey was conducted by and culled from www.oasis.com

[84] Fraud 'Directly Related' to Financial Crisis Probed By JASON RYAN, ABC News Report, Feb. 11, 2009

[85] http://refuge.org.uk/get-help-now/what-is-domestic-violence/domestic-violence-the-facts/

[86] http://refuge.org.uk/get-help-now/what-is-domestic-violence/domestic-violence-the-facts/

[87] http://www.womensaid.org.uk/domestic_violence_topic.asp?section=0001000100220036&itemTitle=Statistics

[88] http://refuge.org.uk/get-help-now/what-is-domestic-violence/domestic-violence-the-facts/

[89] http://refuge.org.uk/get-help-now/what-is-domestic-violence/domestic-violence-the-facts/

[90] Clinton, Tim, Dr. & Hawkins, Ron, Dr., (2009) *The Quick reference Guide to Biblical Counselling*, Baker Books

[91] http://alcoholism.about.com/cs/costs/a/aa980415.htm

[92] http://www.cdc.gov/nchs/data/nvsr/nvsr56/nvsr56_10.pdf

[93] http://www.blazinggrace.org/cms/bg/pornstats

[94] http://www.problemgambling.com/faq.html

[95] As reported by in The Sun newspaper, Women's health section, 16 August 2007

[96] http://www.jesus-is savior.com/False%20Religions/Wicca%20&%20Witchcraft/teens_and_witchcraft.htm

[97] http://en.wikipedia.org/wiki/Claims_to_be_the_fastest-growing_religion

[98] http://enjoyyourmarriage.com/home/63-book-teasers?start=1

[99] Dr. D. K. Olukoya "When the deliverer needs deliverance"

[100] Olaiya, P.J.A, Rev., *Smashing the forces of evil*

[101] http://www.bbc.co.uk/music/artists/569c0d90-28dd-413b-83e4-aaa7c27e667b

SOME OTHER PUBLICATIONS

BY DR SOLA FOLA-ALADE

**21 WAYS TO
MIND YOUR
OWN BUSINESS
(VOLUME 1)**

**SO WHO DO YOU
REALLY THINK
YOU ARE?**

**DISCOVER YOUR
HIDDEN
TREASURES**

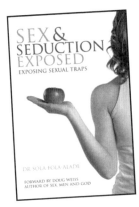

**SEX &
SEDUCTION
EXPOSED**
EXPOSING SEXUAL TRAITS

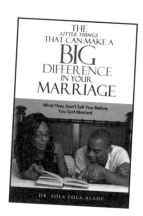

**THE LITTLE THINGS
THAT CAN MAKE A
BIG DIFFERENCE IN
YOUR MARRIAGE**

LEADERSHIP & LIFESTYLE MAGAZINE

Visit www.developingleaders.net

Diagnostic Tools
By Dr Sola Fola-Alade

MARRIAGE CHECK UP
How Healthy is Your Marriage?

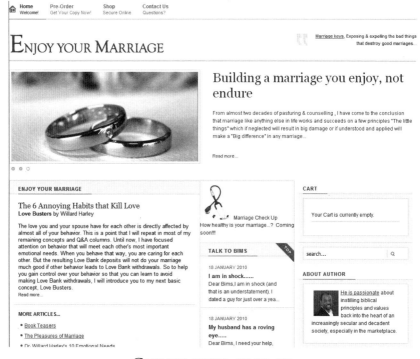

CHECK THIS OUT AT
WWW.ENJOYYOURMARRIAGE.COM

Spiritual Warfare Profile
(WWW.EMPOWERMENTUNIVERSITY.COM)

AUDIO SERIES

BY DR SOLA FOLA-ALADE

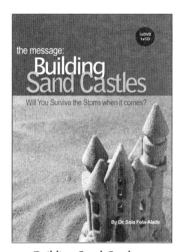

Building Sand Castles
(CD &DVD)

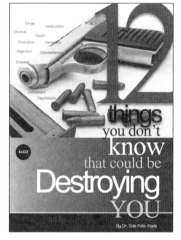

12 Things you don't know that
could be destroying you
(4 x CD)

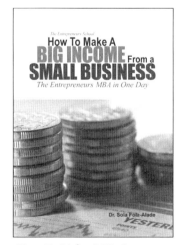

How To Make A Big Income
From A Small Business; The
Entrepreneurs MBA in One Day
(6x CD)

Living on the Cutting Edge
(30 x Mini Sermons)